BIPOLAR:
Living with it.

Memoirs of my experiences of
living with this condition.

Ian Higgins

ISBN: 9781925284041

Cover design: Emma Higgins

This book is dedicated to:

Barbara, my wife,

Bronwyn our daughter and Geoffrey our son,

their partners, Stephen and Peta-Anne

as well as

our grandchildren:

Emma and Naomi,

Eloise, Sascha, Charlotte,

Saul and Imogen,

and my brother Shane;

whose love, each in their own way,

has enriched my life.

Right to this very day.

TABLE OF CONTENTS

PREFACE

I followed what I think is a usual procedure in writing the Preface, only after the book was written. So, it became eventually not so much a prelaid plan, as a path into unexpected places. My initial ideas kept evolving into various transformations: the later transmogrifications almost unrecognisable from earlier forms.

These are my memoirs of a lifelong journey viewed from a bipolar perspective. Consequently these words do not constitute an autobiography. Rather, I am seeing my moments and learning along the journey in a bipolar way. It is through a landscape littered with personal experiences, literary fragments and rocks; all well scattered. This is a journey through what I have found to be a wonderful, sometimes mysterious, terrain of gentle undulating plains, old residual volcanic trachyte cores, as well as unexpected escarpments with their slowly rising slopes and steep black basaltic cliffs.

This is my country, imagined and realistic, in a Don Quixotic way. Maybe it can resemble an Australian Aboriginal Dreaming country. However it is conceptualised in white fella outsider ways. "Country" for the Indigenous people is a living encapsulation of the whole environment: human and physical, stars, earth, sky and all the creatures, great and small, that can be alive now, as well as the spirits of the ancestors and the mega fauna in Dreaming stories. Some of this we consider, as children of the European Enlightenment, to be so mythological as to be unbelievable. To me this remains as more of a mystery. I share with Aboriginal traditional culture that all country is sacred. However in some very significant places the sacred is stronger, more focussed, than elsewhere.

So much of my bipolar musings in this wordy text, including reflections along the way, are saturated with many words, but they may be rather light on the expression of human emotions. As I write in a conversational, manic-depressive way, the style can be described as my version of a stream of consciousness writing, which includes the repetition of stories from time to time.

A chance discovery in the Rockhampton City Library of a person relating their experience of a bipolar condition and using their paintings to conceptualise it, enabled me to realise how I could write my memoirs from my bipolar perspective. These could be in prose and on occasions, poetry, interwoven to form the fabric of this text. My poetry is usually in free verse form or "worse". Only very occasionally do I use stylised rhyming patterns, which are like those we invariably had in our *Queensland School Readers* in the 1940s. Unfortunately when I do write this "proper" poetry, I worry that it could be doggerel. Who knows? The multiple ways readers read and interpret can be quite a mystery. It would be possible to read only the poetry, or only the prose, if only one of these is your preference.

Before I completed the whole draft manuscript, I did not research academic texts. In editing along the way I would sometimes check the correct wording of a quotation, if it could be traced. Initially all quotations and allusions came out of my memory, which remembers, forgets, and even creates, Mediaeval God-like out of nothing (*ex nihilo*, being the theological Latin for this). I followed a procedure enunciated by Gerard Murnane, who wrote somewhere that if one of his ideas, or life events, didn't remain embedded in his memory, then for him presumably it was of no great importance or significance.

I have been helped over the last two years by psychiatrists, psychologists and psychiatric nurses from Peninsula Health on the Mornington Peninsula. I have also received regular counselling by Steve a psychologist at Positive Psychology in Mornington. Without their help and also my family, I could not have made this journey and still be in good spirits for whatever may emerge along my road into the future.

In a sentence, this book is looking at the experience of living with a bipolar condition through a "bipolar lens".

Ian Higgins, Mornington Peninsula, February 2020

CHAPTER I

THE UNFORESEEN EVENT

Christmas 2016 was a difficult time for me. I tried to do all the right things, say nothing inappropriate, put others first and not become overexcited in various social engagements. Maybe all contributed to my undoing: going into a slump when the festive season was over. In late January at the doctor's surgery, this conversation occurred.

> He said, "You are depressed."
> "Oh! No I'm not! Just a little down."
> "I beg to differ. You need some antidepressant pills"

These were duly prescribed and, as you do with a course of antibiotics, I began to take the whole course, day by day as prescribed. Day by day I became more energised and the depression quickly faded away. I had a lot of what my mother always called, "get up and go." And every day I became more intense. I kept talking more incessantly, wrote on a whiteboard in a higgledy piggledy way the ever growing plethora of tasks I intended to achieve.

Then one night in late January, when I was on the phone to a long-time friend, he asked to speak to my wife, which he did and said words to the effect that she needed to ring 000. She replied that she could not. So, he did and organised the relevant person at "000". After her call, the ambos duly arrived, gave me an injection and some pills to settle me down. They informed my wife that I should now go quieter and go to sleep, but they would come again if necessary. Four hours later, around 2am, I was still awake, high as a kite. Once again Barbara rang 000 and the ambulance duly arrived.

"You need to come with us to the hospital."
"I am not going in an ambulance to any hospital."

This suggestion of going in an ambulance reminded me of my last time in an ambulance over fifty years earlier, speeding through the suburbs of Brisbane, Rocklea and up Annerley Road, the siren blaring, taking my mother to hospital. Mum had taken an overdose of sleeping pills, the empty bottle being left beside the bed. When I tried to wake her up for breakfast I found she was unconscious, from which she would never awaken.

Now this night, so many decades later, the paramedics said,
"You have to go."
"No! I will not go. Take me in a police car if you like."

They gave me an injection to settle me down and reluctantly in a daze, I went off in the ambulance to Emergency at Frankston Hospital.

Next morning I awoke presumably in a ward for those patients who are to be taken to another ward, or maybe I was still in the Emergency Ward. All I recollect was a nurse saying to me something like,
"Now you are awake, you can have an injection and breakfast."
"I am happy for breakfast: but I don't want an injection."
"You can't have breakfast, unless you first have an injection."
"Well I'm happy to skip both."
"That is not an option."

So a nurse came to inject me. I pushed the nurse away. Then two came. I did the same. Then four nurses appeared. A big male nurse quickly turned me over onto my face. I was jabbed from behind, in my behind.

I woke up hours later in a room by myself. Later I would discover I was in the Aged Persons Mental Health Unit.

As I had private health cover that the public hospital could claim, if I was agreeable, I had the option of a private room. This would later prove to be a godsend, as I could retreat there into my privacy.

At first I was rather dopey, as the staff experimented with various medications to lessen my ups and downs.

One day I found where they kept the white board markers and the rub out "duster".

Each morning on the white board in the Common Room was written the date, the weather for the day as well as any special events. I wiped out the lot and in its place wrote words in Spanish, Arabic, Hebrew and Greek, using the appropriate script. The staff left these there for some days. During that time a visitor to another patient talked with me about the meaning of these words. Eventually my interests moved on and the board was returned to its usual use.

I found the regular daily routine rather boring: too predictable for a person of my temperament. It was like being on an interminably long distance flight; the monotony of the hours punctuated by food and drink coming on a trolley along the aisles: breakfast, morning tea, lunch, afternoon tea, dinner, supper. As the fuggy drug induced haze began to clear, I ruminated about strategies to overcome the daily boredom.

I soon discovered I was under lock, but not key, rather there was a numbered pad on the wall beside the exit door. For fifty years and more, as parish minister or chaplain, I had visited many patients in such places. I was always told the correct number sequence, followed by the hash key to open the doors. Now I was like a refugee on Manus Island, to be detained indefinitely. My circumstances were so much better, but for me, there would not be knowledge of the magic words "Open Sesame!"

Sometime around this time, a psychiatrist informed me that I had been diagnosed as having experienced a "Late Onset Bipolar Event". The team were trying, by trial and error, to get my medication in the right balance. Once achieved, this would lesson my up and down extremes.

I was informed that, as I was an involuntary patient, it would be necessary for me eventually to go before a tribunal to determine when I would be released. Things were beginning to look a little grim.

> O the mind, mind has mountains; cliffs of fall
> Frightful, sheer, no-man-fathomed. Hold them cheap
> May who ne'er hung there. Nor does long our small
> Durance deal with that steep or deep...
> Gerard Manley Hopkins, *No Worst*

In the hospital I rediscovered a very important aspect of my coping with the relentless restlessness of my condition. Unless I am lethargically depressed, I become immersed in reading and writing. Finding a way with words has been a real contributor for my consolation and my salvation, as I will discuss further on.

Late in life my interest has been increasingly focussed on the words of poetry. Free verse is the form most appealing to me. The word patterns do not have the constraints of a fixed number of syllables to a line, the necessity for a fairly regular metrical pattern, such as iambic pentameter. Nor is there the need to sacrifice a quite apposite word for a lesser one which just fits the rhyme.

As mentioned in the Preface, recently I discovered, by chance in the Rockhampton Public Library, a most helpful autobiographical book by a person surviving her bipolar melt down. On the way to recovery, she discovered painting to be her medium. Through painting in her own rather abstract style, she could express her experiences as they unfolded. In the book she had interwoven her prose text with examples of her paintings as she narrated her story. Later on this would help me recount my memories in my two preferred media: poetry and prose.

LONGING FOR FREEDOM

However at that time in the Mental Health Unit one overwhelming desire evoked from my being under lock and key was longing to be free. I recalled memorable words which begin a speech by Don Quixote to Sancho Panza, "Freedom is the greatest gift God gives to human kind."

Also there came back to mind words I had memorised on seeing the Epitaph of Jonathan Swift in Saint Patrick's Cathedral, Dublin. Now best known for his *Gulliver's Travels*, Swift was Dean of the Cathedral. He wrote his own epitaph in Latin. I learned off by heart an English translation, which I could recall in the hospital.

Here lies the body of
Jonathan Swift
Doctor of Divinity,
Dean of this Cathedral,
Where strong indignation
Can no longer
Lacerate his heart.
Go traveller,
And if you can,
Emulate one who
Strove for
Liberty.

All I wanted was my liberty! As I experienced deprivation of liberty, I came to even more intensely abhor our country's support for the detention of refugees. Sometimes still, during the night, it gets me down. I have marched in protests, written to Members of Parliament, but votes are more important than compassion, even for those politicians who very publicly declare they are Christians. Appalling! And my imprisonment was indeed indefinite, but thankfully I had friends and family who could visit every day. A very caring staff sought to stabilise my mood swings and my release was possibly not too far away: but when? Oh when?

One morning the sun shone strong and from my bedroom window I could see the summer clear blue sky, with no dust haze or cloud, I felt with a sense of desolation, I am "cabin'd, cribbed and confined" within these walls. I can sometimes go out into the high fenced garden, if I can get permission to go there from the one who holds the keys to open the magic door, which is normally strong lock-bolted shut.

In a moment of epiphany, I saw so clearly: this is no other than the Brisbane Grammar School, circa nineteen fifty four. I am now so strangely there: the old school revisited! just "deja vu... again!" as the comedian said. However unlike my time there in the nineteen fifties, I was now a boarder, a real Grammarian: no longer one of those "Dagos", which was the title the boarders conferred on the "day goers" who walked out of the school grounds after half past three, while the boarders remained confined to barracks.

Some years earlier I had learned of a similar experience but of far greater intensity. The Jesuit Dan Berrigan had been incarcerated for his public opposition to the Vietnam War. He was jailed and began wasting away because of brutal in-prison treatment. Father Berrigan was eventually released, only after the Pope's personal pleading with the US President.

Once years later I heard him recite poems about his prison experience, when he visited Melbourne. Later Dan Berrigan gave public readings of various poems he wrote during that time. Two dominant themes were: the overwhelming desire for freedom and the obsession with time, as he was doing time, wasting time, indefinite time.

TIME

I began to realise that my being locked up in this unit was going to be rather longer than the few days I had expected. I needed to develop strategies, not just for survival, but also for living well inside. This had to be more than just enjoying the good food that always came hot if intended to be that way. It was not my thing to watch endless television programs on commercial channels dedicated to consumerism.

Reading and writing have always been important to me. From early childhood, "dreamy Daniel" as Mum would say, since I had a propensity to retreat into my imagination, wandering around the yard or through the portals of a book.

In the hospital ward for the elderly I began writing my day-to-day journal, some of which would eventually prove to be unintelligible. I was obviously in a worse space mentally than I can now recall. Later I would write more comprehensible words about this period, which along with my concerns for freedom also focussed on the awareness of time. Many timely and untimely variations and associations came to mind. I remembered the words of a popular hymn written by Isaac Watts, "Oh God our help in ages past":

Time like an ever flowing stream,
bears all of us away;
we fly forgotten as a dream
dies at the opening day.

Then like Dan Berrigan I reflected a lot about various aspects of time:

Doing time. Wasting time
Times out of joint,
Lost time. Time like a snail
Time's winged chariot
Never passing near.

Time for rest and recreation.
But who wants that
In the lock-up?
Free time?

But I am serving time
In this penitentiary
How long will this time be?

No timeless land in here:
Rather time saturated.

But maybe this present time
Could be blessing,
As well as curse.

Time to be thankful?
For this time to look
Back in time?
Maybe understand time past?
Gain some wisdom?
Hope for a future time?
A time of new experience?

But one timely question
Persists, aggravates,
At what time
Will they ever say?
"Now it's time for you
To go!
The door is open wide!
To that new time.
You imagine so!"

CELEBRATE DESPITE

Because I am aware of how relentlessly time goes so slow in here, I decide I have to seize the time: or even better still, brighten up the time in detention: lest I lose hope. I can turn each day into a special day, rather as in Spanish culture, where there is at least one saint for each day of the year.

I create *The Green Frog Day*. Family visitors bring in my stuffed green frogs and chocolate frogs for afternoon tea. I recall frog stories, which I made up and told so many years ago in a school, where students wore froggy green uniforms.

Then *The Don Quixote Day* with my home-made Don Quixote hat with that circular piece cut out of the brim for holding by hand, because it was in fact a barber's bowl used for letting blood. I recall stories of Don Quixote: his delusions and strange insights being rather appropriate for life in my new abode.

The best day of all is my *Mad Hatter's Party Day*. It takes planning and discretion to acquire food; mainly different biscuits for morning and afternoon tea, not brought from the far away kitchen, but kept in a pantry beside our eating area. As the Unit has the outside garden to help in the healing processes, if a patient goes out there, it is compulsory to wear a hat provided by the hospital. These are of various sizes and designs. So I collect some of these, put them under the bed, 'til my wife and daughter come for this unexpected party.

The Mad Hatter's Party Day begins with style: each of us with a hat on. There is one of my small wombats for the imaginary tea pot. No dormouse is available, but in earlier research for a University of the Third Age course I presented, I had discovered that more than one literary critic claimed the dormouse in the teapot had been inspired by a pet wombat wandering over the dinner table in the home of the Pre-Raphaelite Rossettis, when Lewis Carroll was dining there. I do have a stuffed wombat available for this occasion.

My wife Barbara is concerned about this event. My daughter, Bronwyn stays in the spirit of the occasion. She encourages Barbara to do likewise. From time to time a staff member looks in to check that all is well.

Some days later in a counselling session about getting the pill balance right, I notice in the psychiatrist's file that there is an extensive entry about my festival events. It dawns that if I keep staging these special performances, I might stay longer inside than I ever want to. The *Mad Hatter's Party* is the last and most hilarious festival day that I will celebrate within these walls.

GO QUIETER ON MY WAY

After that, with the obligatory hat on, I went into the sun-saturated garden to weed and water. When inside, I began to ride the exercise bike; kilometres to nowhere: boring as this may be. In the privacy of my room, I could read and write to my heart's content. Unknowingly then, I now believe, this reading and writing contributed to my becoming more settled, though when I tried to later read what I'd written, so much seemed incomprehensible. Obviously I was not in a good state then.

Reading and writing, if not bicycle riding, have always helped me to settle down, to keep the darkness from rising in my soul. When I was out in the more communal places I sought to be the very model of a truly placid person: this being my idea of how to be seen as, 'normal' in this rather abnormal situation.

18

And as a supplement to the reading and writing, on a lucky day I might even manage to change the TV from a commercial station to the SBS or the ABC!

Throughout the hospitalisation, family and close friends frequently visited me, but on later occasions I only recall some of these. Along with family and close friends, a Hospital Chaplain and our local Parish Minister, Paul Chalson came. Both conversed with me in life affirming ways. The concern of all these people expressed in their actually visiting must have significantly assisted my journey to a recovery from the extreme moods which had plagued me.

CHAPTER II

AT LAST

After three weeks of treatment, which was primarily concerned with finding the most appropriate medication, I was allowed to go home. My understanding of my life had been changed utterly. What had been denied by me, or had never occurred to me, became so very clear.

It had not been an easy road, but one I am so glad to have walked, even though this has been rather late in life at seventy-nine years old. The experience reminded me of a quotation Prime Minister Malcolm Fraser once made and then lived to see it repeated often in a truncated misleading way. I expressed my feelings in this poem:

"Life was not meant
to be easy",
But that's not all
the PM said.
He went on to say
the full quotation:
"but take courage.
it can be delightful"

Even at this time
of re-evaluating
all that went before.
Wisdom can come
in so many ways,
after a B-P event.

Don Quixote also
quotes an old proverb:
words we all know
"When one door shuts,
another opens "

Once again,
the quote truncated.
Fully declares,
"One door shuts,
another opens.
One door shuts,
another shuts.
One door opens,
another shuts.
One door opens
another opens too."

The wisdom is,
Fast find the open door!

Do not hesitate.
Seize that open door!
It won't stay open
for evermore.

For me a new door had opened. It was a portal into both my
past and towards the future. It was indeed a Janus-like
experience, but it can be hard to believe that I had indeed not
only had a late onset bipolar event, but I have actually lived a
bipolar existence for as long as I can remember. Still I
sometimes wonder, "Will I one day wake up and see the

diagnosis of having this condition as permanent is in reality an allusion?" My counsellor over the past two years assures me the diagnosis is without any doubt; whether I like it or not. Also he concurs with the psychiatrists at the Frankston Hospital, that I have a heavy genetic inheritance.

My task now is to continue in my acceptance of the double regime of medication and counselling, so that I may stay on a more level trajectory and gain insight into my disability, even though I find that word distasteful. And this has involved a change of lifestyle.

> The old boat nearly eighty,
> sails on tattered and torn,
> though the hull a little leaky
> it still must sail on:
> still go between
> the Scylla of elevation and
> the Charybdis of depression,
> with the help of Epilim.

THE RIGID RITUAL REGIME

A key element to keep sailing on and not becoming shipwrecked is to follow a rigid ritual before going to bed and after waking up. The ritualistic behaviour saves me from going down in a depression direction in the mid-morning. I think this has been as crucial as always taking my medicine at the appropriately prescribed times every day.

The self-imposed regime which I have adopted after counselling, is quite easy to comprehend and can be conceived as a set of **Commandments for Life,** for my bipolar condition. These are my parody in many ways of the Ten

Commandments including their preamble in the Bible. Their divine origin is highly problematic, and they do sound rather daggy (to use good old Australian slang), but they work for me , dislike them as I do.

Following ancient Biblical practice, the day begins at night-time, as it is written in one of the stories of creation, "And the evening and the morning were the first day." (Genesis I:5b)

Having been delivered from a place of bondage: Thou shalt remember that thou wast once a prisoner in a mental health unit; until you were set free to live again in a land that floweth with wine and honey, called the Mornington Peninsula on Port Phillip Bay.

1.Thou shalt go to bed only for sleeping. (Not protracted pre-sleep reading, or complicated cogitations.)

2.Thou shalt have enough sleep.

3.Thou shalt do some stretching exercises, on awakening.

4.Thou shalt remember to go to the loo and empty thy bowels.

5.Thou shalt have a hot shower.

6.Thou shalt eat breakfast at a regular time.

7. Thou shalt not forsake a mug of coffee at this propitious time.

8. Thou shalt do what is right and good in taking thy prescribed medication, regularly, as long as thou live in the land given you.

9. Thou shalt straightway after breakfast embark on a brisk walk around the neighbourhood, usually towards the Flock Coffee Shop in Dava Drive.

10. When thou walkest in the coffee shop way, thou shalt remember to observe the birds of the air and the flowers upon the earth and so be glad that a new day has dawned again.

CHAPTER III

BEING A LIFELONG STRANGER

One of the consequences of my reflecting on my hospitalisation has been an awareness that I have always felt a bit out of kilter, a stranger in the land. Often in conversations of a serious nature my mind goes off in many directions that others find hard to follow, or possibly do not wish to do so. Also as I grew up as a teenager said I wanted to become a minster of religion, this seemed to delineate my being a stranger in the family, especially a dominant section of my mother's family.

As a child and teenager, whereas my peers were so interested in various sporting activities, I was into ideas. These were wide ranging: geological, literary, philosophical and theological, along with an intense curiosity about the worlds of nature. Mum sometimes accused me of being a "dreamy Daniel", which I was. However I had other associations with the name Daniel. Engraved in my mind was an old Sunday School attendance stamp with a picture of Daniel, fearlessly surrounded by lions in the lions' den. So the epithet actually appealed to me in more than one way. Daniel was alone and he was courageous as well. I would like to be that too. I still recall that children's poem beginning, "Dare to be a Daniel, dare to stand alone!"

My own experience is encapsulated in the following free-verse text in which I have used the third tense, "he" for myself.

As long as he could remember,
he was a stranger:
somehow different.
Flowers, rocks, birds,
spoke to him.

The shimmer of an electric blue dragonfly,
wings translucent in the sun:
orange and black of the butterfly's
open shut wings against the sky.

Others did not hear,
voices of the Aboriginal ancestors
in the trees,
beside the White Pioneers' graves.

Somehow he saw things
at an acute angle,
quite oblique.

One song spoke to his soul.
Just one phrase,
"The Stranger from Galilee."
He too was a stranger
from somewhere else.

CHAPTER IV

CARING COMMUNITIES

While I have always felt in some ways a little different, with interests my peers often did not share. My wife Barbara has been a sharer in these areas. All our married life Barbara has been a caring companion, though for many years we did not guess that some of my unusual behaviour was in fact an expression of bipolarity in my personality and often not directly related to what was going on outside of me.

Along with Barbara as the years passed the most important caring community for me became our extended family: our daughter Bronwyn, son Geoff and then moving out to all those named in the Dedication. To use the title of a film popular with teenagers some decades ago, they were always prepared to, "Stand by Me", through thick and thin. They have been a web of support holding me up. Without them, I do not know how I could have coped, particularly as I grew older.

Yet I know there are those with a bipolar disability whose family have for various reasons moved away because they couldn't cope. It became all too much for them. Yet to be deserted by loved ones must be a desolating experience for many; especially if, as it sometimes seems, "They never really understood what bipolar is."

Close friends are also very important for me. I imagine they can take the pressure off family members who can find some aspects of my bipolar behaviour quite wearing.

There is also a multitude of community organisations which have the potential to be supportive. However, regrettably our culture has become more individualistic over my lifetime. In the Mornington neighbourhood this has symbolic expression in the erecting of many high fences. Whereas once fences were quite low, many made of a wire webbing "see through" nature. Clubs and Church congregations in previous decades flourished. Now they struggle for members. Yet it says in the Good Book in a way that prefigures insights from social psychology, "It is not good for the earthling to live alone." (Genesis 2:18)

Throughout my life church communities have been very supportive. Many members of our local Uniting Church see an essential aspect of a Christian faith, no matter what their denominational past, to be active carers of another in need. This is indeed quite a different form of Christianity from those traditions, which enforce uniformity of belief and behaviour, which in turn can be boundary-enforcing of a cruel and destructive nature, as in the ancient saying, "So much good done in the name of religion: so much evil".

At this retired stage of my life, the University of the Third Age (U3A) has been important, providing for companionship in the sharing of ideas and discovering new learnings. It has also given me the opportunity to be creative in designing courses and presenting them as a tutor in our local U3A.

Despite all the community support, sometimes the well-intentioned do not really believe that the bipolar condition is biologically determined. They come up with their own solutions, gravitating around my need to act on my own volition and do something about it. There is a strong ideological individualism rampant now in our Australian culture, which includes the belief that any person can become what they want to be. The large billboard advertising one Victorian university includes the assertion, "You can be what you want to be." Our current Australian Prime Minister Scott Morrison believes in "A fair go for all who have a go." The onus is placed on the individual to have a go. A corollary is, if you don't get where you would like to be, it's your fault, you're just not hungry enough.

This is a rebirthing of the 19th century poem by William Ernest (sic!) Henley, *Invictus*, which was used to badge the recent Disabled Veterans Games.

It matters not how straight the gate
How charged with punishments the scroll,
I am the master of my fate,
I am the captain of my soul.

Over my lifetime I have been told to take control of my emotions and my moods. As a child it came as, "Stop being a sook." "Just sit still!", "Stop talking!", "Don't interrupt!" Later in life the suggestions come in modified forms, but still there often is the assumption that it is about time I got over it and acted normally.

CHAPTER V

LOOKING BACK WITH DIFFERENT EYES

It took many months to realise that my experience of this bipolar event would give me new perspectives on my past life, which would facilitate my becoming aware of bipolar elements, which previously I had not noticed, or denied. A contributing factor may have been that my mother suffered from an intense (hyper) bipolar disorder. Hers was often more severe than any depression or elation, I experienced. Also as a child growing up in a home saturated with Mum's bipolar behaviour, I thought this to be fairly normal.

In my opinion the lives of so many of the neighbours were simply very dull indeed. No parents around us used colourful words like Mum did. No other kids went on adventures with their Mum like my brother Shane and myself. You never knew when Mum would decide to take us on our next adventure – in the train, or plane – to somewhere else. We went to celebrate New Year at Kings Cross in Sydney, where our Gran was managing a boarding house in Kings Cross Road. For school holidays we did not stay at home. We were off in the rail motor to Beaudesert and then into the Lamington National Park. Other times we were off in the steam train to Nambour, then down to Noosa on an ancient sugar cane train; other times by steam train to Southport on the South Coast (now the Gold Coast). Even on weekends, straight after school on Friday afternoon, we went off to stay at Wellington Point beside Moreton Bay.

We simply lived with Mum's ups and downs. A most unusual thing for us was that she was a widow, a single mum. There were no other children of single mums in our neighbourhood, or at our school that I ever knew about. Sometimes she got the opprobrium of neighbours and the wider family for not staying at home and being a 'good' mother: always going here there and everywhere too much. Good mothers stayed at home, did housework, did not beetle off to town on a sunny day, but did the washing. And they certainly did not have rowdy cocktail parties from time to time, which went on into the early hours of the morning.

That Mum was a manic depressive person and that I might be one too, never dawned upon me until I was at the University of Queensland, and over 18 years old.

ELEMENTS OF A BIPOLAR CONDITION, WHICH I SHARE

The philosopher Wittgenstein once said that some things cannot be defined by a simple definition. Quite complex entities may come, each one with a slightly different collection of certain elements. In some cases, every element may be present; in others only some. From my discussions, life experience, and general reading, I feel that in my case there can be some frequently occurring bipolar elements, which I have not experienced. Other aspects, or characteristics I do have.

RISK TAKING: A GREAT TEMPTATION

One of the clear elements, in my version of a bipolar condition, which has been of continued concern to both psychiatrists and psychologists treating me, is my propensity for risk taking.

Ever since I was a little child, I was a risk taker: always willing to, "do a dare". I always had to be the most dare-devilish member of the group I was in at that time. As a teenager in the local church youth group, the P.F.A. (Presbyterian Fellowship of Australia), I rose to the challenge to see who could jump from the highest point off a cliff into deep water. I exceeded all the other dare devils there. On a youth group tour to the Crosbie Dam, we stopped below the dam, beside a bridge over the flooded Brisbane River. I alone jumped off the bridge into the turbulent muddy river below. I struggled out about a kilometre downstream. Fortunately I had not been impaled on a snag or sucked below the surface and pinned underneath one. I was so happy about my achievement, oblivious to the dangers.

Decades later, I walked off the path too near the edge of the rim at Kings Canyon, despite our Indigenous guide warning us against this. When he was concentrating on some endemic shrub, I had my chance to look closely over the edge into the canyon below. When almost to the edge, I slipped in the gravel. I dug my elbows hard into the ground, came to a stop, my legs dangling over the abyss. Little dislodged pebbles clattered down into the deeps below. The guide then pulled me back and up, safe and sound. He said not, "I told you so!" but rather generously, "This is your lucky day!"

A most disturbing aspect of this behaviour is the irrationality of it all. In the mid-sixties I was a 27 year old Presbyterian Minister in Goondiwindi. From time to time I conducted funerals for young men who had been driving often in excess of 160 ks, as in those days the magic macho speed was exceeding 100 miles an hour. To hurtle along at that speed, or more, was energising. However failing to beat the train on the crossing could be fatal: so too a tyre blow-out, a sudden kangaroo, cattle straying across the road, or a skid on the gravel bend into a telegraph pole or gum tree.

If there is no unexpected mishap, you just low fly. The road opens up magically, rather like opening the lid of a tin of fruit with the now outmoded tin-opener, or quickly unzipping a garment. Despite my conducting these funerals for young male drivers, which often included all the passengers in the car, I still would drive sometimes around 160 ks/hour (i.e. 100 miles per hour) or even well over this magical 160 on the long, unsealed sections of the road from Goondiwindi to Moree, a distance of 127 ks.

The list of my multiple risk taking escapades could boringly go on. Once a friend who has a quick way with words, remarked on one of my stupid risk-taking activities on the very edge of a cliff, "He's courting death." Then added, "I hope one day, he does not marry her." Since the hospitalising "event", I've given up courting her, this last two years.

Now looking back after counselling and my own reflections of times past, I think I must have had a guardian angel.

Only after the "Event" in my seventies, have I taken notice of the advice coming from my healers. I seek to avoid all engagement in risk taking activities. I try not to yield to the temptation to drive over the speed limits. If I am aware of my being elevated or depressed, I do not drive the car.

CHAPTER VI

THE BINARY NATURE OF BIPOLAR DARKNESS

Going into a dark place as people suffering from depression do, has been for me sometimes terrible: other times darkness has been my friend. As children we were brought up in a traditional Queenslander house, which was on high stumps and battened in under the house. The darkness underneath could be a creative place, as well as mysterious and scary. As an adult and a parent moving from Queensland to Victoria in my early thirties, I found it so strange that children in suburban Melbourne often played inside; often in the lounge room, or dining room, as well as in their bedrooms. This was so utterly different from my life as a child in Brisbane.

We never played upstairs. On days when it did not rain, we were out in the yard, on the street, or around the neighbourhood: sometimes roaming far and wide, the only requirement being, "You have to be home before dark." If it was pouring heavy, subtropical rain, then we were banished to under the house. Only, "sitting still" games such as Ludo, Snakes and Ladders, or reading a book, were allowed upstairs. On very cloudy dark days, underneath the house could be quite dark, not to mention swarming with mosquitoes.

Yet this sometimes rather dark place could be a wonderful place to be. We could dig channels to make our rivers by diverting rain in gutters from outside in the yard to flow under the house. There we could create our fantasy cities, assemble a geological collection, and forage through all the discarded stuff put under the house, "in case it might come in handy sometime". So if I was not depressed the darkness there could be my friend. And it could be a creative place to be. I wonder if other persons with a bipolar condition feel likewise.

Creative darkness is a minor but important tradition within that collection of various scrolls we call the Bible. This is particularly true of the Hebrew Bible. In the well known Adam and Eve creation myth, "the Earthling" (H-ADAM) is split into male and female in the darkness of sleep, to become "Earthy" (ADAM) and Eve (HWH) "Life Giving".

When Solomon dedicates the Temple in Jerusalem, he goes into the place that is the symbolic expression of the Divine presence. This is not a realm of dazzling light: rather a place of deep darkness. In the text there is a fragment of a poem, which includes the words, "The Lord has said that he would dwell in thick darkness." (I Kings 8:12)

It is also interesting to realise that the Authorised Version translation and virtually all subsequent English translations of the Hebrew text for Psalm 23, the phrase "Valley of Death". In Hebrew it could be literally "a place of deep darkness". So the translation could be, "Though I walk through the valley of deep darkness, I will fear no evil" (Psalm 23:4)

Committed to lifelong learning, it seems I have taken an almost lifelong time to catch onto some things, even those which may have been part of my life for as long as I can remember. One of these is that having to travel through the deep darkness can be the way to what is wonderful. Buried deep in our minds can be those mysterious realms of our imagination.

A most enthralling section of the *Epic of Gilgamesh* deals vividly with Gilgamesh having to go through the dark on his quest to discover the secret of his life renewed. He comes to the mountains of Mashu: to the gates into the mountains and the guards are scorpion creatures, half human, half scorpion. After negotiations Gilgamesh is allowed to enter and goes into the deep darkness within the mountains. There is "the darkness ahead and darkness behind and no light" for league after league, until suddenly he is in the Garden of the Gods. This is not much like the one in early Genesis but rather like another Biblical Garden of Eden story, which is described in Ezekiel 28, where there are stones of fire and trees bearing jewelled fruit: sapphires, rubies, carnelian and lapis lazuli.

Like Gilgamesh, I would love to have my life renewed so that I could be young again. Like him I discover that will never be.

However I can go on various journeys – real and imaginary – to quite wonderful places, even if sometimes the way is through the dark.

Sometimes in the small hours of the morning, I have thoughts that become poems, or become sections of this story. On occasions I need to get up and write these down. Other times they remain able to be recalled to the surface of my mind, on awaking next morning.

Contrariwise the darkness of oppressive depression is a very different darkness: not only dark but as well, a slowing down in the dark experience. As an adult, not long before my late onset, I had the depressing experience of having the difficulty of putting one foot after the other, feeling cold, as well as slowing down. There was the haunting memory of a hymn I learned as a child with its sad statement that, "many kinds of darkness in this world abound". This is a strange, awful obverse to my, so much more public energy, and my sometimes talking endlessly, stringing on story after story.

At this moment of writing I find it difficult to recall just how awful some periods of depression have been, when anxieties proliferated in my mind. All underwritten with a fear that my most loved ones might find me all a bit too much to live with. The fear of rejection can be very strong. And there is that inability to, "just get over it" by doing something, like going for a walk or thinking positive thoughts, or stopping seeing everything to be so negative". All requests or directives are utterly impossible to act upon at that time.

I believe it could be not uncommon for persons who suffer from depression, to effectively hide this from so many people. Sometimes it is only the immediate family and a close friend or two, who know. The depressed person simply withdraws out of sight, until the depression lifts.

As a teenager, I thought being depressed was quite normal. When John Woolcock, a close friend, said that he never got depressed, I did not believe him. I thought his words were just macho male talk. Even just two years ago, when my GP and my wife, Barbara said I was depressed, I rigorously denied this. As a psychologist friend of mine once said, "Denial can be a wonderful cloak of self protection: a great way of avoiding the pain of self-awareness."

Today in a local magazine, while waiting for a doctor's appointment, I read of a person saying that her time of prolonged and deep depression had become a gift to her. Only after experiencing this time did she come to fully appreciate the wonder and mystery of life more intensely. On reflection I feel this is indeed wonderful for her, as she never mentioned any recurrence of depression. However for a bipolar person, even one who is getting counselling and taking the prescribed medication, there can always be the spectre of a shadowy doubt, wondering when the next depression will set in. Certainly family members seeing the increasing, or sustained period of elevation can become concerned as to just how long will it be before a crash down into depression.

But how can I avoid the dark from swallowing me? One strategy that can work is reading voraciously, which I have done for as long as I can remember. Somehow this activity can take me somewhere else. My preference is very much non-realistic fiction. So many popular books in our secular, empirical culture do not achieve this. I find long descriptive realist depictions plain boring. I prefer to immerse myself in the often magic-realism of Spanish-speaking cultures. In my fifties, now thirty years ago, I began studies to read in Spanish. This has greatly enriched my life. Once Jorge Borges, the famous writer from Argentina was quizzed in a radio interview as to the most significant person he had ever met. He replied, "My life would have not been so enriched if I had never met.... (long pause) Don Quixote de La Mancha." I feel the same way.

CHAPTER VII

THE IRREPRESSIBLE ACTOR

Another way of not descending into depression is to perform before an audience, improvising my script rather in the style of Billy Connolly, whose performances change from night to night. Shakespeare's words could be modified when he writes , "All the world's a stage, the men and women merely players", especially if in a bipolar way. And like Billy Connolly, I often do not follow a script written by someone else. Maybe this is encoded in the genes. Whatever, it can come as a bonus if you choose the appropriate profession, as Billy Connolly obviously has done. The family live with this, "for better or for worse". I recall reading somewhere that one morning Billy's partner in exasperation yelled something like, "For Christ's sake Billy, just shut up for once! You are not on the stage! You're supposed to be eating breakfast with your family!" I wonder if he did then go quiet and if so, for how long?

I have been an actor – unaware for most of my life. I got a not exactly late start in Grade 2 at Yeronga State School in Brisbane.

Some thirty years later my moving from parish ministry in the mid-seventies of last century into a college chaplaincy became wonderfully energising, stimulating and challenging. It was to be just right for me, although then I did not know it.

At this stage in life this came out of the blue when the new Principal of a Victorian Uniting Church college rang me up. As

I was a member of the College Council, I naturally assumed this would be about Council business, which it was not. The Chaplain at the junior campus had unexpectedly resigned quite suddenly. The Senior Chaplain of the College, had recommended me as a suitable replacement. So I was appointed. My families' lives were changed irrevocably.

I became aware of this in my first few weeks of teaching Religious Studies (R.S.) in this new environment. One day, the class became distracted by a noisy student sitting in the very back row, which is the perfect place to observe everything that is going on in the classroom and to cause trouble. I lost my patience with his loud mouth interjections. I got so angry with him that for the latter part of the lesson he said naught. Next lesson he was back in full flight making snide remarks to humour his mates. So I said to him later, "What's got into you? Your good behaviour lasted less than thirty minutes!" "Oh" he replied, "I went home and told my Dad about you. Dad said he paid big money for me to come to this school to get a good education. But you need to know that in the world of business religion can be a big handicap: like putting lead in the saddle bags on a good horse. They don't come out winners. He doesn't care how much I muck up in R.S. It is R.S. you know!" Then he added, "My Dad said, If you muck up in English or Maths, I'll give you a belting you won't forget."

This helped me over the years towards understanding a possible reason for some students' belligerent behaviour in my classes and why some parents during parent-teacher interviews indicated they were simply not interested in the Religious Education (R.E.) section of their child's report.

An Aboriginal playwright – whose name I cannot recall – said, "You cannot teach white fellas anything, unless you do it through humour." Much earlier, before I became aware of his words, I wrote an article for the *Australian Journal of Religious Education*, in which I advocated using insights from Bertolt Brecht's perception of how he wrote plays. A crucial element is to assume the audience will be alienated from the beginning. Students in compulsory R.E. can indeed be that.

When I went later to another college as a Chaplain, I had become the great performer: sometimes to the chagrin of good old Methodists who really found it difficult to become involved in the newly emerged Uniting Church in Australia, which brought together Methodists, Congregationalists and nearly all Presbyterians in Australia, in 1977. Some of these good Methodist teachers got off the church tram once they left school and had little time for new developments, desiring a faith structure that "changest never," which also applied to their understanding of God.

Sometimes, teachers who were Old Collegians, would inform me through variations on the theme: that Dr Wood, the Methodist Principal of their teenage times, would never do what I did! "And you call it worship!"

I did not care in a purely insensitive, bipolar style, when someone's anger "made me" a little more manic, I could become more elevated. Sometimes their unsolicited contributions were like the gift of a rising thermal to a wedge-tailed eagle, enabling me to fly ever higher, higher, on a gyre of increasing energy: quite uplifting, contrary to their intentions.

41

Other times I was quite grounded, in an unpredictable way, so much so that some colleagues thought I was rather eccentric. Fortunately in that educational environment, I had the freedom to write my script and depart from it whenever the Spirit moved.

What more freedom would a person with a bipolar condition want? So it could be a pleasure and challenge to devise my own liturgy, only using a lectionary or prescribed prayer book as a source for ideas and sometimes structure. This could be a great gift when celebrating interfaith weddings of Old Collegians. These could be, a Christian and Jewish wedding at the Melbourne Zoo, a Muslim and Christian marriage in a college chapel or my participation in a Greek Orthodox funeral.

Within the Christian traditions sometimes those involved were devout Catholics but were happy to be married by someone they knew. They wished to have a say as to what they wanted in the service; rather than being offered a set menu.

THE IMAGINED PROPHET: ADVOCATING JUSTICE

As a teenager I was attracted to the lives and words of those I regarded as prophets, not in the sense of foreseeing the times to come: so much as speaking out against injustice and seeking to do something about this in their day.

In the First Testament of the Bible, Amos who spoke up so fearlessly for the poor provokes the wrath of the king and is told to just go somewhere else,

"O seer. Just Go! Flee to the land of Judah. Earn your bread there, and prophesy there. Never again prophesy at Bethel, because it is the king's sanctuary and it is a temple of the kingdom." (Amos 7:12)

Jesus said enigmatically, alluding to the emblems on the standards of the Roman military, "Where the corpses are there will the eagles gather." (Luke 17:38) And there remains his caustic, often misunderstood remark, about giving to God what belongs to God and to Caesar what belongs to Caesar. (Mark 12:17) As a Rabbi said, these words are like holding up money with Hitler's face on it in Occupied Denmark and saying sarcastically, "Give to Hitler what belongs to Hitler. Give to God what belongs to God." The Rabbi added, "Such people often are executed, as I believe Jesus was."

So it seems those in power can assume they are beyond contradiction and hate those who threaten the status quo, which is structured to their advantage. As a Chaplain, I found this could be true for Principals and Heads of School who felt their way was the only way. When I believed a student or staff member was being unjustly treated, I had no compunction in confronting those in authority. When confronted, they would sometimes change into would be tyrants. On more than one occasion I was threatened with being "encouraged" to move on to a position that, "better fitted my undoubted gifts". Presumably in a bipolar way the threats hardly touched me, as I was elevated by the energy being generated in the interaction. Threats could be like water off my duck's back. Sometimes my remarks bore positive fruit and the person was no longer treated unjustly. Sadly at other times, to use a phrase from Seamus Heaney, "I threw the stones of silence".

CHAPTER VIII

EMOTIONAL DISCONNECTION

My own self protection which shielded me from the anger of another, could have been an emotional disconnectedness. Now I realise that over decades my inner moods and responses did not connect with what was happening outside me. This can be a gift when another person is in serious trouble, or when I'm dealing with some catastrophe. Then I can be very helpful, because I am not overwhelmed by what is happening.

I have not always been courageous, failing on one occasion to stand up to an angry customs officer in Cairns International Airport, who was harassing my wife for not declaring some item that she did not remember had to be declared. I still feel sad at times about this failure of mine. Although Barbara said quite definitely she does not want me to keep dwelling on it.

There is also another disconcerting aspect to this disconnectedness. I can be in a happy mood when I should be in a different emotional space, because of the unhappiness of others who are present. And then this can go in the other way, upside down. Even in my preteens, I found myself at one of my own birthday parties unable to be happy, though others were enjoying themselves immensely. I knew Mum had done everything she could to make it such a very happy occasion: yet I was depressed, just wanting to be alone. So I went off to be by myself, wandering in the deep shade of a big tree in our front yard.

In moments of self-awareness, along with the memories of sad events well past, I can be vividly aware of this emotional disconnection. I can unexpectedly become on the verge of tears: the sudden pain so deep, the past lack of appropriate emotion; now so unrectifiable. This is then re-engraved in the unalterable past....doesn't matter how interpreted or minimised by me now.

As teenagers in the nineteen fifties, my brother Shane and I would play over and over again, on our very avant-garde record player, Edith Piaf singing, *Non, je ne regrette rien* (No! I have no regrets!) I still love to hear her, now on YouTube. However I do have many regrets; not the least of which has been my insensitivity and unawareness of the pain of others on occasions at the actual time of their suffering.

Since the "Event" and my subsequent imprisonment in the Aged Persons Mental Health Unit at Frankston Hospital, many once-buried memories of my emotional disconnection rose unbidden in my mind. These could occur at any time, day or night....after midnight was the worst time.

When we were married, Barbara expected to be loved and cared for. I was often unaware of my inability to respond appropriately to her needs for expressions of affection.

Once recently our daughter Bronwyn pointed out that even now, when Barbara and I are at a social event, I am up and off: relating to anyone and anybody, all over the place, telling stories and, conversing enthusiastically. Barbara would be left high and dry to fend for herself. Bronwyn added that other couples at the dining table from time to time glanced lovingly at each other, "but you don't do that."

Early in the time when I was the Minster of the Presbyterian Church in Goondiwindi when the congregation sang about, "our loved ones and our best". Sitting in Church, Barb expected me to glance at her from the pulpit; yet I did not even look in her direction.

Now I have to consciously try to be aware of her, more expressive of concern for her needs. It can be very hard not to feel fake, because the expression of affection does not come easily or naturally to me. It is hard to know if this is part of my condition or my socialisation. On an occasion when I spoke to my mother about her nursing me as a baby, she responded, "The Black Boys did that."

At least in these latter years with Barbara, I can attempt to be more sensitive to her needs, even if I can't change anything about the past. With my mother it is so different; never to be put right: only learned from, painfully.

One early evening when I was 27, I arrived home at Corinda, having driven down from Goondiwindi, about 400km from Brisbane. Mum wanted me to stay and talk with her. I had another agenda. Deaf to her needs, I said I had to go and see some friends at Graceville and so I did. When I got home it was rather late and Mum had gone to bed. Without disturbing her, I also went to bed.

She failed to appear for breakfast the next morning. Going into her bedroom, I found her unconscious, an empty sleeping pill bottle on her bedside table. I ran next door to the Cecils, rang for the ambulance, who came almost immediately. We headed off with the siren screaming across Rocklea flats, up through Annerley and on to the hospital.

On the weekend I returned to Goondiwindi, because I felt I was needed for Sunday Services. On Monday I drove again to Brisbane, unlocked the front door and picked up an envelope shoved under the door. It read, "So sad about Cilla, Uncle Bob." I ran over to see Uncle Hal, Mum's brother next door. Holding the telegram in my hand, he said simply, "She has passed away."

I don't remember much more of that sad time, other than Barbara flying from Sydney to be with me. She stayed next door at the Cecils.

Later I would see on Mum's Death Certificate the stated cause of death was pneumonia, which was the convention of the day. It makes me wonder when it is stated these days, that suicide was less common decades ago, was this so? Or is it as one historian said succinctly, "How would you know, if it is not in the documents?"

Over many years as a Parish Minister, and as a College Chaplain, I conducted hundreds of funerals. This was the time before the advent of Australian Civil Celebrants. At that time, theologically-liberal compassionate Ministers or Priests became the celebrants in virtually every funeral and wedding in the community.

I remember tiny white coffins for little children, once a line up of eight coffins for three generations of a family who had crammed into a large car and whose driver sought to beat the fast moving Western Mail Express over a level crossing outside Dalby. Later as a Uniting Church College Chaplain, I conducted funerals for students and staff members known to me who had committed suicide. I could do these without shedding a tear. So I was seen as very professional and I assumed I was.

Now I believe that some unknown proportion of my "professionalism" was in fact associated with my bipolar condition. Also the more bizarre and tragic, the more likely my manic side was expressed in energy and creativity. As I wanted the service to be accessible to all who would be present, almost every prayer, in fact nearly all my words in a funeral service were of my making, except the traditional "ashes to ashes: dust to dust". Only in very tragic deaths did I use the oft quoted words attributed to Jesus, "Blessed are those who mourn, for they shall be comforted." If the deceased had experienced a long life I was inclined to add another of his beatitudes, "Blessed are those who mourn, for they shall laugh".

Ironically, being on a bipolar spectrum could mean that any service of worship, which, I conducted could take unexpected turns. This could offend those who were rigidly ritualistic in traditional ways. In Dromana Uniting Church at the turn of the century, a retired Minister who had become an uncomfortable pew sitter, sought me out after a service to say, "You'd do so much better, if you had a set order of service and followed it." He was less than impressed when I said I did have an order of service but it just kept changing along the way. Such an impromptu style could be challenging for the organist.

This fluid style of life was also what my wife Barbara had to live with for the fifty four years of our married life.

CHAPTER IX

THE VORACIOUS READER

Stories have been so important to me all the days I can remember; certainly from when I was five years old. That year Dad died and earlier that year he had given me a book called *Cuthbert the Caterpillar and Wilfred the Wasp*. In the front he had written, *Ian Lindsay Higgins 1-1-1943* in green auditors' ink indicative of the occupation he had before the War in New Guinea.

After Dad died, in mid 1943, I found comfort in bright flowers, clouds and butterflies and above all else, the stories which I heard in school or Sunday School. Eventually I could read whatever I liked all by myself. Mum allowed me to read anything I wanted. She was quite marvellous in that way.

Some of the Biblical stories are quite macabre: like Samson tearing apart a lion and later pulling down the pillars of the Philistine building, or Jeremiah who would not shut up even after the King told him to do so. For his troubles they put Jeremiah down into a well. He sank into the mire. Once I nearly fell through the rotten wooden cover of a disused well. This was nightmare-producing. Still I kept reading.

In Grade Five on one happy day, our class teacher at our Sherwood State School announced that the Government was giving each class a little library to be housed on two shelves. In this mini-library I came upon a green covered book with gold writing, which read, *Treasure Island* by Robert Louis Stevenson. So I became Jim Hawkins and ever after set out on many voyages in the good ship *Hispaniola* and met many a Long John Silver on the way.

Now on the wall above my desk is a photocopy of a page, copied from a colour plate in a volume of *Richard's Topical Encyclopedia*. Uncle Bob had given us this twenty-volume encyclopaedia sent in order to "broaden our knowledge". He was like Mum in this educational way and very generous.

The colour plate is of a piece of embroidery with a short poem above a sailing ship in full sail. The words, which I learned by heart so long ago are:

A Ship is a Breath of Romance
That Carries us Miles Away
And a Book is a Ship of Fancy
That Can Sail on any Day.

Since then,

Much have I travelled in the realms of gold
And many goodly states and kingdoms seen
which fealty to Apollo hold.

Certain books have remained engraved in my memory long after my reading them. These have become guides for my life journey: some well suited to my bipolar condition. Perhaps none more so than *The Wind in the Willows* which tells of Mum's favourite character Mr Toad, who also resonates with me. He is the consummate risk-taker, which is expressed in fearless most manic ways. When Toad, the escapee from the prison in a washer woman's clothes, steals a car and drives off in a most "elevated" way, "a little faster; then faster still, and faster. Ho! Ho! I am the Toad, the motorcar snatcher, the prison-breaker, the Toad who always escapes!"

Such selecting of a hero must be a family trait, as Aunty Roma chose Becky Sharp from *Vanity Fair* as her model and named her tearooms after her.

As a child, I was attracted to Don Quixote, whose windmills' story first appealed to my imagination in a *Queensland School Reader*. Like Don Quixote, I am a dreamer from early on: but then, as was the case in the wanderings of Don Quixote, a "Sancho Panza" appeared in the form of my wife Barbara who Sancho-like still brings some of my dreams back to reality.

However my "quixotic identification" is in a consciously imaginary way, which is rather important to say, as when I was questioned by the outpatients medical team from Frankston Hospital, I was regularly questioned as to whether I was hearing voices. I had to assure them I was not.

SEDIMENTARY STORIES

So many childhood stories
embedded in my mind;
some even metamorphosed,
the limestone into marble.

That radio serial story
nightly on the ABC
The Search for the Golden Boomerang
Now transmogrified to be,
the Aboriginal dreaming story
The boy's lost boomerang
transformed to be
golden blossoms
on the silky oak tree.

I see again so vividly
the pier of life's journey
from here out towards
a far horizon,
along which all humans walk,
broken decking, here and there,
through which some people fall
some even pushed
as they walk this way,
and eventually all of us
fall
into the sea,
swept away
by the swift,
tides of time.

As in *Kidnapped*
I climb rickety outside stairs
Nearly step into
a fatal plunge
only a lightning flash
saves my life,
just in time.

Sail again on the *Hispaniola*
seek my Treasure Island
find another has found
the treasure buried there.

Set off down the road:
Cuthbert the Caterpillar
And Wilfred the Wasp:
along with me
on a journey
of fantasy to see
the wide world,
mystery in the mundane,
and eventually
the welcome lights,
family and home.

CHAPTER X

THE COLOUR-FULL EYES

Earlier this morning I had a not uncommon experience for the bipolar-seeing person. Today I was particularly conscious of this, because it had rained heavily overnight and in the morning light, the sun burned bright in a clear, blue sky. Dew drops were sparkling on the Victorian winter emerald grasses. The trees seemed to be silvery alight. Then as I drove through a patch of Ironbarks with their black trunks, a flock of white cockatoos alighted on the grass with uplifted sulphur crests: a colourful contrast to the black bark on the trunks and their bright white shapes strong in the green grass.

This intense awareness of colour has been with me all my life….one of those wonderful gifts to a person on a bipolar spectrum.

As I drove along I remembered a scene I witnessed in the National Gallery of Art East Building in Washington, D.C. While I was contemplating another work of modern art I can no longer recall, along came a group of kindergarten children and their teacher. They suddenly saw Jackson Pollock's *Lavender Mist*. They were transfixed. "Look Miss!" "Look Miss!" they cried. I too was transfixed. Somehow the variegated lavender and purple colours spoke to my soul. As long as I live and still am *compos mentis,* I will remember this painting. I have the same feeling about *Blue Poles*, housed in the National Gallery of Australia thanks to Gough Whitlam and to the chagrin of some art-loving Americans I once met at a dinner party in San Francisco. They said something about my coming from the country that took the America's Cup from them. Actually that did not matter much to them. What upset them was our acquiring, *Blue Poles*. "It should never have left the USA!"

THE GARDENER

While I have never experienced actual voices in my head, many aspects of nature, as well as colour variation in plants and creatures certainly "speak to me". After my Dad died, when I was five, I enjoyed going out into the garden at our wartime home at the corner of Wilkie and Green Streets, Yeerongpilly in Brisbane. In that subtropical climate winters were invariably mild, except when a cold westerly wind blew from far inland. In the subtropical climate bright flowers could flourish all through the year. Yellow flowers lifted my spirits.

Just as I loved getting out of the house into the garden; even better was to walk up the street, looking at the dazzling white-topped cumulonimbus clouds, butterflies of various colours, the multicoloured beds of nasturtiums, bright red hibiscus flowers and the heavily scented frangipani.

I still am delighted now over eighty years later to see colourful tropical and subtropical flowers.

I find it easy to resonate with and to follow those words that conclude Voltaire's *Candide*, "Il fait cultiver notre jardin." I have found it very important to cultivate our garden and cannot imagine living contentedly in a dormitory house with no front yard or back yard large enough for gardening.

I do not know whether the enjoyment and life-giving aspects of gardening are derived from my Mother's socialisation, or a response to my bipolar condition, maybe both. Such things may be impossible to know. However being out in the garden or walking through the bush both settle my spirit and wake me up in a way that just quietly sitting, listening to another person can rarely do.

THE CARPENTER

Similarly more recently I have found pleasure in resurrecting my skills in woodworking, which I learned at primary school, on Thursday afternoons in the Milton State School. Around midday as a class totally unescorted by a teacher, we strolled up Sherwood Road to the station, got on the train and half an hour later got off at Milton, beside the hops-smelling brewery. We walked to the State School, where as boys we learned woodwork and metalwork; while the girls did domestic science.

The idea of going to a Men's Shed – as is common for many retired Australian men – does not appeal to me very much at all, because I do not feel comfortable in male only groups. Again this could stem from my early life experience during the War, living and in a world where males rarely appeared and women were always present.

THE COOK

I have loved cooking ever since a family friend, Hazle Jessup gave me her recipe for "lemon curd" which I discovered is the Scots word for what we call lemon butter. I was surprised that on the very first occasion I made this, I got instant praise: so different from teaching where praise or appreciation may take years or never happen. This cooking experience got me on my way and I still enjoy cooking very much indeed.

As a digression, as I typed this I remembered a student at a twenty year reunion of Old Collegians who came up to me and said, "I always wanted to thank you for helping me understand the meaning of life." I was somewhat surprised at this but said naught at that moment. Then she added, "My brother went to another school. He doesn't even understand the jokes in *Life of Brian*. I love all the Monty Python films." So it goes.

But back to cooking. As the plethora of television cooking shows indicate, cooking can have a large element of acting as well as cooking. On reflection I am in agreement with *The Age* journalist Jamila Rizvi who wrote that, whereas yoga and meditation did not still her churning mind, cooking did. However for me there still can be a manic rushing around the stove and kitchen to coordinate all that may be cooking. In the bipolar way, I can have the freedom to be creative. I do not have to slavishly follow the listing of ingredients, or the suggested procedures for cooking.

CHAPTER XI

THE ORANGE LIGHTS ARE FLASHING

In his poem *To a Louse*, (1786) Robbie Burns wrote:
O wad some Pow'r the giftie gie us.
To see oursels as ithers see us!

With these words in my mind at the beginning of 2019 I began to wonder: how do others see a person with a bipolar condition? I began consulting my friends and family and questioning how they could see that I have a bipolar condition, or to use the old phrase, manic-depressive condition.

For those who did recognise this, indicators to them included my propensity to use many words in a torrent; not ever sitting still for more than a few moments; and interrupting others while they are speaking and have not yet finished what they intended to say. Sometimes it is the impulsive remark which others may well think, but dare not utter, as this would violate a social convention. Interestingly all these indicators could have been descriptions of my mother's behaviour as well.

Some of the insightful responses included:

"I knew from around the late seventies. Also it's easy to pick as you start talking and go on and on."

"I never noticed it; never knew till you told me. When you come into the shop for your regular coffee kick, I think you are just always bright and happy, always prepared to tell another joke."

"You just won't stop talking."

"You don't give anyone else a chance to speak. When I suggest you give someone else a go, you just go on, as if you never heard."

"You're a terrible interrupter."

And so on….

THE NIGHTMARES

There is a hidden enigmatic aspect that they can never observe, namely my nightmares. Time and again I have a frequently recurring nightmare. I am in a car, hurtling down a highway with the accelerator jammed. The brakes won't work. Sometimes I am driving through ever deepening fog, or the windscreen turns opaque, or I become totally blind. Usually I manage to avoid other vehicles on the road. At some point I wake up feeling utterly exhausted and disoriented, with a myriad of thoughts buzzing around in my head.

Once I can remember a significantly different unfolding. In this dream I go off the road while speeding uncontrollably around a bend with the ocean far below. The last thing I do with terrible sadness is say to Barbara, who is in the car beside me, "Goodbye." Even typing this brings tears into my eyes….the very thought of this. Naturally when I awake, it is as if I am in the film *The Castle* and the Dad says, "You're dreaming!" However it is not easy to undream such a dream and go back to sleep.

Usually interpretations of dreams are of doubtful validity. Maybe not for all of them. Once when relating a version of not being able to stop the careering car ever accelerating down the road, a school counsellor thought the dream expressed how I appeared to be to him and other staff members. Of course because denial, or ignorance, can be a great self-protection from what we do not want to acknowledge, I saw this as just another opinion, not necessarily a valid insight.

Some early mornings about four am, I have horrifying dreams. I wake up: cannot go back to sleep, because a myriad of worries, imagined and real, begin accelerating the whirlpool of my mind sucking me further into that maelstrom. A Panadol may help, but usually I remain only half asleep, drowning in my worries. I know that I will awake in the morning, possibly with a mild headache and certainly in a very depressed mood, which may start to fade by midday. In the meanwhile I worry that I am letting Barbara down by not being in a level place and not being able to face enthusiastically whatever we had planned for the day. She is mostly understanding.

I am still trying to deal with this by talking with my counsellor, Steven. I do not seem to be able to get over it.

CHAPTER XII

WELL INTENTIONED HELPERS THAT MAY NOT UNDERSTAND

Recently in a U3A tutorial group, I made some allusion to having a bipolar disorder. Someone quashed my comment by saying in a tart voice, "That was so last year." After this imposed full stop, the discussion went elsewhere. Too bad the poet Byron under consideration appeared to have a hyper-bipolar condition. A problem is that some people find discussions of mental health issues uncomfortable. Their attitude can be summed up in variations on a statement said to me on more than one occasion, "Let's not go there."

Trouble is, once you've been diagnosed, you tend to become more aware of others who appear to suffer the same condition with its blessings and curses: even though some of them also will not want to go there, even vigorously deny it. Nevertheless it is not always easy to stay silent. Well I have never found that easy!

As with a number of mental conditions in our culture, the bipolar one often cannot be easily talked about unlike some other medical conditions like a heart attack, dementia, diabetes, or obesity, to name a few. Mental conditions that are seen as 'not normal' are not the best dinner table items for conversation. In one dinner group that I attend, I have sought on numerous occasions to talk about my bipolar condition, to no avail. As our once Prime Minister John Howard said, with regard to dealing with those who did not see things his way and with whom he had no intention to interact: "Just treat them with silence…. So very effective."

More recently depression has come more into the public limelight. However very little attention, seems to be given to the manic side of those who are on a bipolar spectrum.

To say to such a person in an elevated mood, "Just slow down!" is a bit like them stepping out onto the railway line in front of an express train and waving a red flag. Steven, who has given me months of psychological counselling said, "It can be rather like telling a diabetic just to lower their blood sugar levels. There is an unawareness that this is something biological." My conclusion is that this cannot be solved the *Invictus* way. It is not "just will power".

So it seems that many of my friends and acquaintances imagine that my experiencing a bipolar event was like catching the common cold, or the latest bad virus. Given time you are supposed to get it out of the system and show the evidence of that, in fulfilment of the media delusional experience, "closure" or "just move on".

Sadly there will never be any closure. It is "for the term of my natural life". If I go off the medication, and eschew the counselling, I will most likely be back on the trip to mania and depression, which may well go from bad to worse.

In fact some who have had no medication and presumably no counselling, can contemplate suicide, and may even do so. Some highly creative people have apparently done so. We have only to remember the poet, Sylvia Plath….and that painter of bright yellow sunflowers and purple irises, Vincent van Gogh. I also remember one of my university friends, who was brilliant in his chosen field of medicine. A few months ago I read in *The Age* he had committed suicide. He had achieved fame and fortune in his occupational life becoming a high-flying chief executive officer. I still wonder, did he ever receive help for his condition: or did he just keep going with his obvious manic energy? This was how his behaviour sixty years earlier appeared to me, that is when we were University of Queensland friends. After his suicide I read a biography of his family. It seemed quite clear to me that he suffered from a bipolar condition. It also emerged in my reading of the text that this was never recognised by his parents, or the sibling who wrote the book.

TRYING TO BE SELF-HELPING

The medical team at Frankston Hospital, reinforced by my psychologist counsellor, gave me good advice when they said not only should I get sufficient sleep each night, but also, to prevent my going down towards a depressive state, I should go for a brisk walk right after breakfast. To the best of my ability and weather permitting, I have sought to do so ever since. Usually this practice works very well and lifts my spirit, even on a dull, grey day.

As far as can I recollect from the fragments of my memories, I have so often been wanting to be on the go, unless I am glum and deenergised. Whenever a teacher at the Sherwood State School sought someone to "run a message for me", I shot up my hand and as quickly as I could, not infrequently reinforcing this by declaring loudly, "I will!" In Grade 7, when Mr Woodgate our teacher, forgot to bring his glasses – which happened often – I offered so enthusiastically that soon I became his chosen messenger: always being asked, "Please get my glasses, Ian" And so I would: pedalling furiously up Sherwood Road to his home. Other times the tasks were more mundane, collecting rubbish, shovelling sand out of clogged-up drains, even hosing down the boys' latrine, a job with a unique aroma. Any job would do rather than sitting still in the hot, stuffy afternoon classroom thinking of the lines from a poem in our Reader:

> A cloud of dust on the long white road
> and the teams go creeping on
> inch by inch with their weary load

I am a very verbal person coming from a family valuing words. So when I have to be still, whether I like it or not, I adopt a wordy procedure to keep the deep darkness at bay. This is through writing: both prose and poetry. When I am liable in conversation to talk far too much, I resort to writing notes in a pocket notebook. When I do this note taking, it can be difficult at times to reassure the others that I am not recording their words: rather I am writing down ideas that keep bee-like, buzzing around in my head. The only way to stop the buzzing is to get it down on paper. I consume a lot of notebooks. So much so that when family and friends are short of ideas for a gift, I am often given another good quality notebook.

Still the procedure of taking a brisk walk after breakfast seems to be the most effective way to minimise the likelihood of my going into a slump, or elevation, after breakfast. Previously, the going down after breakfast happened so often once we were retired, I thought it to be a natural feature of ageing. I would feel so lethargic and down that I would collapse into a comfy lounge chair and go off to sleep to get my energy back.

Going on the after brekky walk, unless there are some interesting plants, clouds, birds or butterflies, I drift off in to fantasy lands....off into the jungle again. Suddenly a multitude of ideas come to birth and take flight, not necessarily to disappear. More like some swallows down the street in summertime, these ideas go swirling and circling around in my mind. Often there emerge wild verbal or visual associations. On occasion I get stuck in a chain reaction of ideas and I move into a subtropical climate reverie, as if I am back in Warwick or Brisbane, as I was so long ago.

A cloud small as a human hand
appears in the sky,
as if from nowhere.
Lightning flash,
Slow thunder rumble.
The late summer grasses
ignite.

Ferocious fires flame forth.
Smoke clouds billow.
Pyrocumulus clouds soar:
dazzling, immense,
high intense, white topped.

Again lightning strikes.

You never know,
when and where
Yet only then
the possibility of a poem
will appear:
a word,
a phrase,
an image,
in that flash.

So transient,
Unless written down.

CHAPTER XIII

IN GOOD COMPANY

Recently an article appeared in a Scottish magazine reporting that researchers at Glasgow University were seeking to ascertain whether Robbie Burns had the bipolar condition. They were meticulously analysing his voluminous correspondence. In one letter he writes, "Half my life is spent in melancholy." The other half, so publicly characteristic of persons with this condition is to be very active and full of energy. Burns' lack of ability to, or maybe lack of interest in, maintaining many close relationships, could also have been an indicator. Actually, from what was in the article, I think there is little doubt Robbie Burns was well on the manic depressive spectrum. As with many other persons like him, he had a way with words.

With Van Gogh the medium was primarily painting. His use of vivid colours reminds me of my mother's use of vivid colours. She used bold colourful designs in her raffia baskets; so unique that years later in a Brisbane street, they were so easy to spot when somebody was walking along with one.

The English writer Virginia Wolf, a wonderful innovator in novels and a strong advocate for women's rights also had a bipolar condition.

Having read a biography of the poet Sylvia Plath, I came to the conclusion that she too suffered from a severe bipolar condition. This was before I read her book *The Bell Jar*.

Virginia Wolf, Sylvia Plath, Vincent van Gogh, and even my beloved mother: everyone such creative people in their differing media and each one committed suicide, presumably in fits of deep depression. Yet Van Gogh's painting still can enrich our lives. Virginia Wolf's writings reveal new ways of constructing a novel. She has also inspired other writers. Gabriel Garcia Marquez somewhere says that his reading of Virginia Wolf's *Mrs Galloway*, was the catalyst for his writing *One Hundred Years of Solitude*, a magic-realistic novel, which has sold millions of copies. My own mother in her modest way not only enriched my life and my brother's in many ways, but also many others into whose lives she brought many words as well as vivid colours.

For me there have been other creative outcomes not restricted to the arts and culture. I have found that some external events can evoke a manic response in me; which can be creative in different ways; particularly if I become angry about some injustice, or other. Sometimes it is the action of someone in a position of power seeking to further their own ends at the expense of others.

In the late seventies I became one of the Chaplains at a girls' school with a student population of around 2,000 students. In the Pastoral Care Unit, there were two Chaplains, two Career Counsellors and two general Student Counsellors. We were located in a beautiful small heritage building, each with our own room. There over the years we made it student and staff friendly, with our memorabilia, choice of paintings and comfy chairs.

On one Easter break, we went away and came back the following Wednesday morning. Our Pastoral Care building had turned into a pile of rubble: broken bricks, smashed up pieces of timber and what was left of the stained glass windows. The other five members of the Pastoral Care Team went into a state of shock: or so it seemed to me. They were stunned.

I immediately, with a great deal of fury and energy, went into crisis management mode. I found where the demolishers had relocated our possessions in cardboard boxes, along with files of confidential information. These were actually in different rooms all over the campus.

At some point the Bursar explained to me this was not done to upset anyone. It was just the best way to get the building and site cleared and ready for a big building project without any objections. His *fait accompli* reminded me of a strategy adopted by Queensland's Premier, Bjelkie Petersen. He would have heritage buildings demolished at around two o'clock in the morning, so by dawn any opposition was rendered ineffective.

Having found out where our items were located, I decided as a group we could take over the first floor of the Year Twelve's Common Room and they could keep the ground floor. I commandeered the school truck and with helpers collected all our items and relocated each of us individually in new rooms with our materials. While returning the truck, the Principal flagged me down. He too was now furious and informed me that I was not the Principal. I had no authority to do what I had done. He added that he too was human and had feelings. I had upset him greatly. For once I said naught. When he had finished his words, I returned the truck to the Maintenance area. And all was well.

CHAPTER XIV

BIPOLAR IMAGES

Strangely there seems to be any number of images, or metaphors, for the depressive side of bipolar, but not so many for the times of heightened elevation. At least I have not come upon too many allusions to the manic. Winston Churchill's use of "the black dog", apparently coined by Samuel Johnson, is well known. Samuel Johnson once wrote in a letter to a friend, "What will you do to keep away the black dog that worries you at home?" Actually it seems the Roman poet Horace used this metaphor a thousand years before. My mother applied a favourite "black metaphor" to one of her relatives, "He's got the black monkey on his back."

As with all metaphors, these black animal ones can be quite appealing to some people. For others it may not be so appealing, especially those who may have a love for a black dog, or like my brother, have a lifelong fascination for monkeys, no matter what the colour.

Interestingly Edward Lear, famous for his limericks and the poem about the owl and the pussycat who went to sea in a pea green boat, was described as suffering from epilepsy. Yet he also had very manic moods, from which he could quickly plunge into depression. He used the colour black for depression and white for his very happy, elevated moods.

Another colour which obviously appeals to others when describing depression, or as they said long ago, melancholy, is to use the colour blue. In recent years in Australia an organisation that deals with depression has the name "Beyond Blue". Robbie Burns spoke of his "Blue Devil". However often in a Victorian winter with days upon days of grey skies, I long for the colour blue, on Port Phillip Bay and in the sky above. Sometimes we drive from Mornington over the low ranges to Bendigo, where often the sky is a bright melancholy-lifting, clear blue. However as one who grew up in Brisbane, the Queensland clear blue sky is best of all for me, as it was for Mum.

As a teenager I came to appreciate another metaphor, which is to be found in, *Pilgrim's Progress:* once one of the most widely read books in English-speaking countries. Early in his journey Pilgrim falls into a bog, "The name of the slough was despond." This falling into the slough of despond occurs on other occasions later in the story.

While these images may be helpful to many, I felt a need to write a poem using my own imagery.

The black dog,
Winston's metaphor,
is not mine:

John Bunyan's much preferred,
the slough of despond
into which I fall
suddenly, unexpectedly,
in the wilderness of this world.

Or now
as I live beside
a southern Bay
It could be
the cold dank mist,
from the grey, fog filled
cold sea:
seeping into my brain,
so soon to be
befuddled utterly.

CHAPTER XV

SAD DAYS
(or Seasonal Affective Disorder Days)

On many occasions my psychologist has told me that my mood swings are not determined by factors outside my mind. However I know that once prolonged grey skies form and come to stay for many cold days, over the Bayside suburbs of Melbourne, the chances are I will succumb to depression: or in more clinical words, suffer from the Seasonal Affective Disorder.

Nowadays despite treatment and counselling and even though I take my pills religiously, I am amazed and sometimes still depressed by the sudden changes in weather in the Melbourne region. I know Jeff Kennett, once the Premier of Victoria, said we should celebrate this wonderful diversity of weather, "four seasons in a day". It is not always easy to do so. The washed-out colours and reduced sky light, can effectively depress me, especially when the grey days drag on for too long.

A New Day Dawns Beside the Bay

A clear blue sky,
Port Phillip Bay,
Colour saturated,
Aquamarine to Prussian blue,
The You Yangs, so clear beyond:

The hot dry North Wind
Gusts hard, all the day,
All the way,
From Broken Hill;
Or is it Alice Springs?

That was yesterday,
Now far, far away

Now we awake,
To a cloud filled sky,
The Bay, silver to metallic grey:
A heavy mist creeps in.
Horizons fade away:
Wind gusts of cold damp air,
From the Southern Ocean.
Cold thin rain falls
In sudden fitful squalls.
Under the grey sky
S.A.D-ness about to descend,
Once again, again.

Light is always important, bright sunlight especially. Even in primary school in reading a section on the lives of famous people in Richard's *Topical Encyclopedia*, I felt that I understood why Goethe called out for "more light" as he was dying.

Regrettably for me, my psychologist reminds me that my ups and downs are to be expected even though I religiously take the prescribed medication. During the early morning on some misty grey days, I wake up in a sludge, feeling utterly de-energised. As the day wears on I become more energised. By evening time when others wish to start settling down for the I am becoming more and more elevated: looking good, clear eyed and liable to become quite active and over talkative. For them this must be a pain. I think the technical name is Diurnal Affective Syndrome. Fortunately for me, my GP Dr. Michael Cross has prescribed some melatonin pills. If I take one of these before 9pm, it settles me down to fall soundly sleep around 10pm.

Sometimes I stay "reasonably" (at least to me, if not my family) elevated for days, even weeks. A series of stimulating events, interesting conversations, and challenging material in a newspaper, maintain and replenish this mood. Going on journeys, especially into the country or overseas, do so likewise.

I love to travel in the spirit of Henry Lawson who somewhere wrote,

> I'm at home and at ease
> on a track that I know not,
> And restless and lost,
> On a road that I know.

I like to choose the road less travelled: much prefer to go where we have never been before, especially bright outback sunlight. This could be an aspect of bipolar, or simply an ingrained wanderlust. Either way, surprises are guaranteed along the new way.

Another awful image of depression comes from my recollecting my being nearly drowned on more than one occasion.

During times when I become "elevated" (as psychologists describe it) this can presage depression. I begin by gently going faster, thinking faster, talking somewhat incessantly, feeling more and more in great spirits. I am filled with enough energy (I believe) to get multiple imagined tasks done quickly. Then suddenly, as in the mythic story, I plunge Icarus-like into the cold deep sea. Then it is as if I have leaden sandals on my feet: an old-time deep-sea diver on the seabed who can scarcely trudge towards the shallows of an imagined shore.

AD PROFUNDUS

I could be Icarus,
my mythic reality:
with wide open wings,
rise higher, ever higher,
nearly touch the sun.

Till wings fall off:
the so sudden plunge,
down, down, ever down,
into the deep, cold, grey, sea.
To cry under water
so dark, so heavy, so soon.

To remain, so deep under,
Could be many long slow days?
or all eternity.
This so awful time.

Apart from almost two years in Rabaul, New Guinea, just after I was born, I spent the next thirty years in Sunny Queensland. The majority of the earlier time was spent in Brisbane. For the last seven years we were on the Darling Downs during a prolonged drought, virtually every day under intense, cloudless, blue skies.

Around five years after marrying Barbara, we went south for a new appointment in Melbourne. On crossing the border into Victoria, even before we got to Wangaratta, I knew (in the Aboriginal sense) I was not in my country. The grass and the lower plants were suddenly too green, the sky a cloudy gloomy grey. Any small patches of blue sky were a paler blue. Apart from the green grass, all other colours were so less intense, so pale in comparison to those in coastal subtropical climes.

As a teenager I read, as was the custom of that time, many books by authors who lived in Britain. Once when I had to write down my nationality on an official government form, I was told, "You write British." In these British books, as in *Prince Caspian* (by C.S. Lewis), ships sailed on silver seas. This seemed strange to me, until I came to live in Bayside, Melbourne. Then I often saw the Bay under heavy grey clouds. When rays of the setting sun came peeping through, the sea would turn a shining silver. Only occasionally was there to be seen the strong Moreton Bay blues replicated on the waters of Port Phillip Bay.

For decades now these cloudy, cold days get me somewhat depressed. This happens especially when the summer solstice in December passes and my idea of a warm breeze on a bright sunlit summer day is arriving in erratic stops and starts.

One cold January, when the hot North Wind did not blow, my depression was so intense I caught a plane to Brisbane. I could walk along beside the khaki Brisbane River in the summer, sunny, humid heat. I went up to the restaurant on top of Mount Coot-tha and with windows all open could watch an intense electrical storm over the mountain caldera far away on the border near Mount Warning. I was no longer depressed. I was rejuvenated.

CHAPTER XVI

CHILDHOOD MEMORIES OF MY MANIC DEPRESSIVE TENDENCIES

One wintry December day in Mornington, Victoria, beside Port Phillip Bay, I felt that deep longing for what the indigenous person would call, "My country".

In the following poem I seek to express my nostalgia in an imagined, child-like way, using the rhyming style, which was so characteristic of many poems in our *Queensland School Readers*. "My country" for me is the whole southern Queensland coastal, subtropical environment. This includes the people there: their ways of speaking and relating, the landscape and seascape, the subtropical plants and creatures, as well as the climatic conditions of the seasons there.

BRISBANE RIVER

Dedicated to Ed and Mai Fryer

> I'd love to be in Brisbane
> Now that spring is there:
> But I am stuck in Mornington.
> Cold grey drizzle fills the air.
>
> But in my mind I go away
> To be beside the River:
> Gaze deeply into khaki depths,
> That still can make me shiver.

Just sit down at *The Rocks,*
To watch
The swirl of life glide by;
To lean upon
a glistening sun warmed stone,
Beneath the wide blue sky.

As far back as I can look into, "the dark backward and abysm of time," (*The Tempest*: I.2.50) in my life, I see precursors of my latent bipolar condition. The Late Onset Bipolar Event in 2017 might have been caused by too many antidepressant pills. Although it was diagnosed "late", it was not, "late onset", It was just a very exaggerated instance of what I had experienced for as long as I can remember.

I have a memory of my three year old self being amazed to see a snail glide over a damp concrete path on silvery slime at the house of Mum's cousins, my maiden great aunts, at St Kilda.

.

When I was six at Yeronga State School, a teacher invited anyone to come out to the front and do something for the whole class. Because of my immediate enthusiasm I was chosen first of all and drew a big elephant on the blackboard. Then I launched into a very loud rendition of my kookaburra laughing. The class loved it. The teacher then explained she wanted only one thing by each student. Why worry? I'd had my go and got to do two things. From then on, I had a taste for performing before an audience. Still to this day any number from one to ten thousand will do.

CHAPTER XVII

SPIRITUALITY AND THE MANIC DEPRESSIVE LIFE JOURNEY

Spirituality, or religion as it was called over seventy years ago, interested me and has done so for as long as I can remember. Possibly my Father's death when I was so young was a deciding factor.

When I was in Form V (now Year 11), I announced. "I am going to be a Presbyterian minister like Mr Ramsay." (Mr Ramsay was our local very well read Presbyterian Minister.) Immediately my Mother on behalf of her Love family and my Higgins' Gran went into a strong mixture of crisis management and damage control, uttering from time-to-time those profoundly rhetorical questions like, "How could you do this to us, when we have done so much for you?"

At a much younger age I could not stay settled and confined in my family tradition, so rational and scientific. Yet in this scientific empirical world I was expected to succeed. It could be architecture, civil engineering or mathematics. The one exception to science which I can recall was the law. These were and would be our family's strengths.

Mum sent me to see the Head Master. She expected him to dissuade me. He did not. He congratulated me and said it would be a hard path to walk, but he admired me for my decision. Mum was not happy. So next I was sent to the careers person in the Repatriation Department who explained that in a secular culture it was not possible to use Commonwealth funds for training clergy. Because of this I would have to study something else, which would be Applied Science in Geology.

The family decision was that I would be allowed to decide for myself after becoming an adult at twenty-one. The family hope and intention was, "One day you will grow out of it, just as your Grandfather, who was a Catholic Priest, did". I never did grow up the way they wanted. Still some relatives and old family friends say words like, "And you had such great potential." "Now you only own a Ford Focus. Doesn't that ever worry you?" Well it did not and does not. My spiritual journey has been wonderful, mysterious and life-giving.

Blocked by Mum and the Repatriation Department from studying to be a minister when I first wanted to, I chose to study the science I enjoyed at university. Yet, after a year studying toward a Bachelor of Applied Science in Geology, I failed two of the subjects: Physics and Inorganic Chemistry. The result was in part due to my spending far too many hours poring over a beautifully bound two volume edition of, *The Works of John Donne: Sermons, Meditations, Poetry and Correspondence*. So, the bell tolled for me. My formal scientific studies were already dead. I could no longer live mainly in this empirical, rational world, "so contracted thus".

Thankfully, it was after only a year of studying science that the Repatriation Department and my Mother relented. With some subjects credited to me, I transferred into the Faculty of Arts at the University of Queensland and after six years, completed my studies to be a Minister of religion.

Almost twenty years later after we had moved to Melbourne, I applied to study Sociology of Religion as a major at Monash University. It was no surprise to hear arguments similar to those of years before about the inevitably fading role of religion in our world. They did allow for pockets of resistance in some unenlightened Middle Eastern and Third World countries and among Indigenous peoples, the latter usually belonging to the academic realm of anthropologists.

At this time, in this academic environment, the emergence of violent religious fundamentalisms was not foreseen or imagined. It would not be too long coming. Actually not only from the desert do prophets come. They can emerge from so-called centres of civilisation: Western and Eastern. They can be Christian, Muslim, Hindu or Buddhist. Now this has happened, lest we forget the fundamental evangelical millions supporting President Trump.

You may wonder how does my approach to spirituality relate to my bipolar condition? I'd say a great deal. But it is not the usual quiescent variety: unless I am depressed there is a relentless restlessness. Not for me those often-quoted words of Saint Augustine of Hippo, "Our souls are restless till we find rest in Thee."

As I grow older my capacity to sit still and listen to another give a talk, becomes more and more difficult. I am so easily bored, unless I can go off in a flight of fancy, out through the claustrophobic doors or windows with my imagination.

It does not much matter whether these ramblings are of great import. It was so clear then to me that I was about to set out on an exciting re-enacting of a story in a picture book given to me by my Father, some months before he died. As in this book, *Cuthbert the Caterpillar and Wilfred the Wasp*, I was off to see the world, to travel as a pilgrim into the realms of mystery, wonder and fantasy. These can be discovered and explored in the vast jungles, deserts, canyons and volcanoes of many religious traditions. Presumably, I will do so till the sunset of my day. Just like a coastal Queensland rainforest, in this region lurk scorpions, red bellied snakes, pythons high up in the canopy. On the path there may be stinging trees and bright red or purple poisonous berries. The sheer diversity is wonderful, awe-inspiring and very dangerous.

The Garden of Eden for me is the coastal Queensland rainforest.

The Rainforest

Under the vast green canopy,
Plants and animals thrive and die
In khaki and green camouflage.

Splashes of vivid colour
Glimpsed now and then,
Plants and creatures,
Not what they may appear to be.

Giant spiders wait on wide nets,
To catch the unwary,
Others lurk on the forest floor,
Amidst the myriad ants.

A frill-neck lizard, mottled bark colour,
Freezes on sapling trunk nearby.
I move. It moves.
Keeps its body out of sight,
Only holds a beady eye on me.
Leeches adhere imperceptibly,
On arm or leg or neck,
Grow black grape size, before they fall,
To leave the slimy bleed behind.

Bright cunjevoi fruit, enticingly
Attractive, crimson poison.

The fresh green leaves,
Of the stinging tree,
To be avoided assiduously.

Pythons hang hidden,
High up in the canopy,
Only come down at night,
Near sightless, seek body heat,
To hunt and strangulate,

Now in this green filtered light of day,
Many creatures move around,
Noisy....out of sight:
Whip-birds, whiiippp, from far away,
Frogs too green to be easily seen,
Croak! Croak! croak! To each other's call:
A rock wallaby, I imagine,
Skitters through leaf mould.

In the fecund humidity,
Water drips, and drips, and drips,
From far green leaves above,
Onto green leaf below;
Thence onto brown and black, leaf decay,
Upon the squishy forest floor.

In the gully,
The living creek gurgles on,
Over boulders in its path,
Black eels wend their way
Against the stream,
In crystal clear cold water.

Time here so indeterminate.

Reaching towards the hidden sunlight,
Beyond the canopy high above,
A massive ancient hoop pine tree,
Araucaria Cunninghamii,
Witness to life in Gondwanaland,
From aeons ago.

White colonial forest clearing,
Black fella burning,
Has not triumphed here.
Strangely the rainforest,
Remains, mysteriously
My soul country,
Land of my dreams.
And my imaginings.

So I entered the rainforest of religion and philosophy. Initially this was a journey primarily through various expressions of Christianity, particularly those Protestant-Eurocentric. At the University it became possible for me to study Comparative Religion, as well as English and Philosophy. After these five years of tertiary studies in many subjects: scientific, religious and literary, I became a Presbyterian Minister in an ecclesiastical culture, derived from the Church of Scotland.

After this my mother always introduced me as, her "little minister", which I believed to be a pejorative diminutive. It was not until late 2018 that I discovered the phrase was another of her literary allusions. *The Little Minister* was the title of a novel, quite popular in the early twentieth century, its author, James Barrie, now remembered most notably for his *Peter Pan* books. In its day *The Little Minister* was popular and was made into three silent films. The main character would have appealed to Mum, because he was a Presbyterian Minister in a Scottish town. In the novel, from time to time, Barrie uses Scots idioms instead of Standard Southern English, in a similar way to the practice of Robbie Burns, another writer oft quoted by my Mother. Sadly I did not find the literary origin of "the Little Minister" until over fifty years after Mum died.

Despite my family's heartfelt concern, even sadness, over my choosing an ill-paid and becoming obsolete profession, I found my six years of tertiary studies stimulating and mind expanding. I enjoyed hearing the often old, old stories embedded in so many world religions. Also I saw the truth of the Ancient Roman adage "So much evil done in the name of religion: so much good done in the name of religion."

I developed what has been a lifelong interest in many of the dominant, and also those marginalised, strands within religious traditions.

For many years I studied Greek and Hebrew languages so as to read Biblical texts in their original languages. Some years later at Goondiwindi, I studied first year French as a distance education student. In Goondiwindi, I did not come across anybody else interested in French language, so I was not very successful in this endeavour. I can still read a French story with enjoyment, but some difficulty.

Decades later 1 was successful in learning Spanish to better appreciate the literature of the Spanish-speaking countries. I found this language to be very interesting in a Christian/spiritual way, because the Enlightenment rationality had less impact on Spanish language writers than in English-speaking countries. Don Quixote and Sancho Panza still wander through the landscapes of my mind.

Through these language studies it became possible for me to journey through many linguistic landscapes, each incarnating a different Weltanschauung (world picture). From my earlier tertiary science studies, the one subject I still explore is geology.

Much have I travelled in the realms of religious gold and dross. Many sacred sites I have seen which, "fealty to others than Apollo, hold" (Keats). So many different gifts from diverse traditions have given me imagined insights not just into "real life" but wisdom as well, I trust.

Unfortunately this seems to be developing into an over long digression. I know in *Tristram Shandy* it is asserted, "Digressions incontestably are the sunshine – they are the life, the soul of reading." I trust mine might be., but best to return to bipolar spiritual themes more explicitly.

In terms of my spiritual ways, times of still, silent contemplation have never jelled with me. I cannot agree with those who advocate meditation as the only sure and certain path to an awareness of the Divine, the Numinous, God, Allah or Nirvana, whichever word you prefer. Again and again in so many traditions of what is popularly termed "spirituality" the basic assumption seems to be invariably: that the first steps involve sitting still, becoming centred and so on, eliminating all distracting thoughts. I find this path impossible to walk. At least in classic Hindu religious traditions there are a number of paths to the imagined divine realms.

Once I visited a forest-dwelling group of Buddhist monks who came from Sri Lanka to live outside Perth. They had various paths through the sclerophyll eucalyptus forest on their site, along which I walked with great enjoyment. I'd term this an experience of the sacred in the Australian bush. There were these massive gum trees with their leaves, which can turn edge-on to the hot sunlight, so letting in dappled light on the forest floor. There were diverse plants. I caught glimpses of creatures, flitting among the branches or crawling along the earth. Then I was informed by one of the monks that my task of meditation was to empty all these images and thoughts out of my consciousness until it was filled with the nothingness, which presages Nirvana. It was not my way.

In fact, always my mind seems to be teeming with thoughts, my imagination often in overdrive. Ways of toning this down can be walking, reading and writing; though all of these procedures are not fail-safe, because they on occasions can become further stimulants to what is swirling around in the maelstrom of my mind.

Reading especially can also take me somewhere else; becoming a portal into the wonderful, mysterious and unexpected. Walking through an interesting landscape I have never seen before can do likewise.

Coming from a Christian tradition, I can well conceive of Jesus of Nazareth as a peripatetic teacher-healer companion. As a teenager a teacher who most represented this style was our geology master at the Brisbane Grammar School. He is immortalised in David Malouf's novel *Johnno*. With "Soapy" Allen, as he was known, we wandered across the Brisbane suburbs observing the geological structures on the surface and speculating as to what might be underground. On one occasion we spent extended time in Lamington National Park wandering along amidst creek boulders and below the spectacular basalt cliffs, relics of a vast volcanic caldera. This was an inspiring learning experience.

CHAPTER XVIII

LIVING WITH A BIPOLAR CONDITION: MY MOTHER, CILLA LOVE

When I was still at the Brisbane Grammar School, I came to know that Mum was, as a psychiatrist said, "manic depressive". The word bipolar was not in use then in the nineteen fifties, to the best of my recollection. So now I believe it is time to relate my life of living with the bipolar disorder of my mother.

One afternoon, when I was in my mid-teens, Mum and I were sitting on the old green painted rustic seat under the mottled shade of the *Cassia Laburnum Fistula* (a golden shower tree). Out of the blue Mum said, "I am going mad!" Suddenly I was observing this two-faced Janus condition, the gift face had flipped over to the curse face. Some months later it was a psychiatrist on Wickham Terrace who spent time explaining to me what it meant for Mum to be diagnosed as a manic depressive person. The treatment was sleeping pills and when it was intense, shock treatment. As far as I recollect the use of lithium had not come onto the accepted medical scene at that time.

Until these words, I thought Mum was normal, just rather unusual, in her behaviour. She was just a little more exaggerated in her behaviour than I was. I saw her times of depression as being caused by sadness over Dad's death, which she really never, "got over". She was more colourful than our neighbours, who seemed dull, rather like the washed-out colours of the often faded weather boards on their houses. Our lives were filled with colourful stories about New Guinea, about the Rabaul region on the New Britain Gazelle Peninsula.

Sometimes Mum's colourful language could be quite embarrassing. Many years after we left New Guinea, Mum would mix up New Guinea Pidgin (now evolved into contemporary Bislama or neo-Melanesian English) and English in her conversations.

Once as we sat in a full compartment in the train steaming towards Nambour she said in her penetrating voice, "Look Ian, Bulmakau!" I thought, "Why can't she just say cows, or cattle?" She never seemed to care what others thought about her unusual choice of words. In some ways in her heart she had never left Rabaul and Kokopo in New Guinea.

However, some years before leaving Brisbane for her new life in New Guinea, she had experienced what she termed a nervous breakdown. The version of this story, which I heard from members of her Love family, began: As a young woman Cilla had a "nervous breakdown". This must have been a deep and prolonged depression. She stopped eating. Her whole body began to close down. She had taken to her bed: refused to eat and began to waste away. The family doctor of some decades did not know what to do.

In desperation a new young doctor in the nearby suburb of Graceville was approached to come to see her and discuss with the family what could be done. He came and agreed she was in danger of dying. He said they needed to find out something that she wanted to do before she died. Eventually it emerged that she wanted to see and hear ocean waves breaking.

Grandpa Love immediately picked her up: put her in his car and drove from the Brisbane suburb of Corinda down to Southport some forty miles away to the nearest accessible surfing area. They went across the Nerang River to the ocean beach under a blue sky, where the roaring waves were breaking, turning into white froth running up the wide golden beach. It was at the height of a king tide. Nothing could have been better. From that moment, Cilla began to recover and resumed her life.

She became the manager of her own linen shop, with many multicoloured fabrics, some of which she would keep in her Glory Box for the rest of her life. The shop was upstairs in the Brisbane Arcade. The onset of the Great Depression of the thirties caused her to close down her business.

Next she came to work as a colleague of Nugent (Nugget) Abell, an importer of expensive and exotic fabrics. All went well until the economy worsened further. Under the economic onslaught of this the new time, demand for expensive imported pieces of material dried up. The reduced income could not support them both.

Mum left in search of alternate employment. Finding nothing in Brisbane to her liking, or matching her abilities, she decided to go further afield. A *Courier Mail* article about her, said euphemistically that Cilla Love was about to "embark on a cruise around the Pacific Islands."

She was actually job searching. The historian Geoffrey Blainey, an Old Wesley Collegian, once said the exodus of so many young persons from Australia to far flung places of the globe is encapsulated in *The Founders Song* still sung by Wesley students some eighty years later in their assemblies. The song includes the words about those who were once students at Wesley College in Melbourne.

> Where grey North waters quiver
> And sun beats fiercely down,
> You'll find Collegians working
> In almost every town
> New York, Canto or 'Frisco
> No matter where you roam.
> You'll meet Old Wesley students
> Ten thousand miles from home.

Mum disembarked at Rabaul, which is on the New Guinea island of New Britain. It was not ten thousand miles from home: rather some sixteen hundred miles from home (2,600 kilometres): though in the minds of many Australians, Rabaul could be the other side of the globe.

Shortly after arrival in Rabaul, she was appointed chief stenographer in the Legislative Assembly. She was a very accomplished shorthand typist and could immediately take down the words uttered in the proceedings and type them up in the equivalent of Australia's *Hansard*. At that time, Rabaul was the Centre of Administration for the Trust Territory of New Guinea.

In Rabaul she met Dad. They were married on the 31st of March 1938. Their honeymoon became their "cruise around Pacific Islands". According to her I was conceived at Port Vila in the then-named New Hebrides.

94

For Mum Rabaul was her Garden of Eden. In her tropical paradise there seemed to be no return to deep depression. Only twice as a child did I hear of her more manic moods in Rabaul. For some reason or other Mum said one day, "When I was talking too much your Dad would say, 'Let's go outside for a cigarette.'" On another occasion when Mum was giving me and my brother, Shane multiple directives, "To do this!" "Do that!" Gran said that she used to drive the native servants crazy by asking them to do a series of tasks, when each one seemed to contradict the previous one.

Decades later I saw this behaviour in a person who seemed to me to be quite high on the bipolar spectrum. This was the Chief Librarian in a College where I was a Chaplain. On one Monday morning she had directed staff to start decorating the library with a *Witches* theme for the week. By recess, when I called in, she had changed this to *Famous Women in Literature*. The staff began to dismantle the bewitching decorations to begin the new task, not too sure what she'd want next. I enjoyed going there when she was having morning tea with her staff. I never knew what she was going to say next: just like my Mum of old, at home in Corinda and presumably in Rabaul.

Late in 1939, Mum's father summoned her to return home and nurse her dying mother. And she did: sailing back to Brisbane on the *MV Macdhui* to nurse her mother who had terminal cancer. I was almost two years old having been born in the Namanula Hospital high up on top of the volcanic rim around Simpson Harbour. This geological formation was a consequence of the collapse of a vast caldera and the ocean flooding in to create Rabaul's harbour.

Once as a child I asked Mum about her nursing me as a baby. She exclaimed with surprise, "I never did. That was a black boy's job. I had more important things to do." Uncle Bob once commented on my strange mixture of English and Pidgin when I got stung with a wasp in Grandpa's garden in Corinda. I said, "A binatang bit me." Sixty years later when Barbara and I went to visit Vanuatu, I felt at ease listening to the radio where the language used was Bislama.

After Mum's Mother died, she sought permission for us to return to Rabaul. This was refused, because a Japanese invasion was expected. The official Australian Government word was, "imminent", which word appears in the official letter refusing to grant permission for us to return to Rabaul.

At this time the Government policy was to deliberately leave behind all the men from Rabaul and in the surrounding region: even though ships were available. The Government in Canberra, preparing for the impending conflict, used the available shipping to transport precious copra. This was to be used in soap manufacture in the U.K. The previously global exporting German factories no longer exported soap to the British Empire.

A subsidiary reason was that civilians behind Japanese lines could be go-betweens with the Japanese and also provide valuable intelligence. Actually some who were not captured did stay. They were often from the New Guinea Volunteer Rifles (the NGVRs) and some patrol officers in other parts of Papua New Guinea invaded by the Japanese. A record of this is in the remarkable autobiography of Peter Ryan's, *Fear Drive My Feet*.

While Mum and I were in Australia, separated from Dad, Rabaul fell to an immense Japanese invasion force on 24th January 1942. The next day a short article, not even on the front page in the *Sydney Morning Herald* read, "Rabaul went silent at 4pm yesterday afternoon." This was before the Fall of Singapore. The silence has largely remained. This is no Kokoda story. It has been consigned to the realm of "historical amnesia" for most Australians.

When the invasion occurred, apart from a few nurses, those captured during wartime just disappeared without a trace. They were mostly civilians: predominantly, planters, public servants and missionaries, along with the New Guinea Volunteer Rifles and the Lark Force, a hastily introduced unit from Australia.

After the ignominious Fall of Rabaul, Rabaul became the headquarters of the Japanese advance through the Pacific. From the underground concrete bunker there in the heart of Rabaul, a few metres from the once flourishing New Guinea Club, Admiral Isoroku Yamamoto directed all operations. The underground bunker with a rusty gate still there, over from the now renovated New Guinea Club, where my mother drank cocktails and the then very popular rum and coca-cola. Served on the verandah: as only males were allowed inside.

One day months after the invasion, we received in the post a formal letter informing us that my father, Lindsay James Higgins was listed as: "Missing Believed Dead." Roughly the same time my Grandfather received an almost identical letter, informing him that his favourite child, Horace Arthur Love, Mum's younger brother, was also: "Missing Believed Dead" in the Middle East.

The months went by so slowly to me as a child. We lived in our wartime rented house, all windows blacked out. Inside, the darkness became deep darkness as Mum became deeply depressed. Gran, a widow and the mother of her only child Lindsay, our father, came to live with us and help out. Time just moved ever so slowly in our rented home, actually half an old classic Queenslander, on the corner of Wilkie and Green Streets, Yeerongpilly in Brisbane.

What we did not know was that some of the NGVRs (New Guinea Volunteer Rifles) had escaped into the jungle and eluded the Japanese in their clean up and execute operations. My father was one of these. Months later he staggered out of the bush into Port Moresby, alone, emaciated beyond recognition, suffering from tinea all over his feet, dysentery and malaria, but still alive.

Dad recovered in the Downland's Military Hospital. Eventually he came to live again with us, only to die eighteen months later in Greenslopes Hospital owing to a "military medical oversight". Fortunately for Mum, he was still "in uniform" and therefore, Mum became a War Widow.

Once again a deep, dark depression fell upon the house. It was already dark in many ways, as every window in the Queenslander was still blacked out because the War was still ongoing. A blacked out house in subtropical Brisbane summertime is not only dark, it is humid and stifling. Outside in the garden I found comfort in bright flowers, especially yellow ones, also the butterflies, the birds and the snow white soaring cumulonimbus clouds.

After the war, when Rabaul was recaptured, many months after the atomic bombing of Hiroshima and Nagasaki, all the Prisoners Of War (P.O.W.s) had disappeared: as well as many expat. Australian civilians. The total number of these, "disappeared" is almost 2,000. This is, in fact, one of Australia's greatest wartime losses, far exceeding the numbers lost on the warship Sydney off Geraldton in Western Australia.

A place of comfort for Mum in her distress was the New Guinea Club, which met in the evening about once a month in town. Here the stories of pre-war Rabaul were shared and became sources of strength, in a wider culture of forgetting.

Some fifty years later I was confronted by the distressed son of one of the disappeared Missionaries from Rabaul. He held a page torn out of what was a philatelist's journal. It was a full page with a photograph of one of the envelopes once containing a letter, which had been written by his P.O.W. father and dropped in a bomb casing during a Japanese air-raid over Darwin. The news about these letters was censored lest this damage the war effort by illustrating a Japanese act of compassion.

The news in the philatelist journal was about the record price for these Japanese occupation stamps. He cried as he said "That was a letter to my mother from Dad. She never received it. She died never knowing her husband as a P.O.W. had written to her." Only the envelope with stamps intact remained: the letter being regarded as of no value, I suppose.

At the end of the War, Mum, with Shane and myself in tow, began hunting for a place where we could live permanently. Once the War Emergency was no longer applicable, the owners of the house we were part-sharing had the legal right to reclaim their occupancy of the whole house.

We went looking all over Brisbane at various depressing possibilities. After one hopeless day of wandering through depressing weatherboards, which had not been painted for almost twenty years, Mum realised she did not want us to continue living in rented accommodation.

Her older brother Uncle Bob, in an act of generosity that still amazes me, gave Mum a block of land. He sold it to her for a peppercorn. Having received this gift, she emerged from her depression. With awakened energy, she began designing our new house, with the help of an architect friend.

We went to live in our new house at 11 Harrowby Street, Corinda. Mum took me down to enrol at Sherwood State School, where she had been a pupil more than thirty years before. In the playground we came across an old teacher of hers, Miss Sparrow. They both began to cry. Through her tears, Miss Sparrow said, "Cilla! I thought you were dead." More tears. At one point Miss Sparrow said, glancing at me, "Does your boy talk incessantly just like you did at school?" Mum assured her that I did not, which was not exactly true.

Once in our own house Mum's creativity and liveliness resurged. My earliest memory of her renewed creativity was her designing and carving a Chinese-style contemporary coffee table, with curved legs. This was made from beautiful polished silky oak timber from a coffin, that mysteriously, "fell off the back of a truck". The coffin timber was given to Mum by a friend. In the early post-War period such wood was very scarce, almost impossible to buy.

Mum's creativity came in great spurts, which could last months. After the carving she made raffia baskets with big bright flowers, like one of her favourite artists Van Gogh. She wore colourful clothes to match her colourful language.

Then Mum moved on to millinery. She would never again use the carving chisels or wooden mallets. They just lay there in the room, later to be put under the house "in case they might come in useful, sometime." For many months she created quite beautiful wide-brimmed slightly floppy women's hats, still to be seen worn by those comfortable, yet nubile well-bosomed, actresses in the films of the time, such as Marilyn Monroe and Jayne Mansfield. Once this interest had passed, the wooden millinery blocks were left in the sunroom, never to be used again.

Next Mum was into pottery. She liked odd shapes and unusual, often very earthy colours. Some of her vases were low rectangular with feet. Another was elliptical, designed for her favourite frangipani flowers.

Gardening, with a focus on flowering shrubs, became the new passion. She planted various varieties of hibiscus: white, lemon, orange, pink and red.

Then came china painting, which did not last very long, as the fumes "got to her" – to use her phrase for what must have been some allergic reaction.

Naturally all this creativity required time. She could not be distracted from her "work" – whatever was the current fascination.

As a child, Mum lived in a house with a live-in maid's room conveniently at the back of the house adjacent to the kitchen.

Day maids would also come to help out. Her mother and presumably my Mother, as far as I could ascertain, never did housework, unless they chose to do so. Mum could cook excellent food, when she was in the mood.

Some years ago Ken Webb whose mother had been a close friend of Mum said, "You know your mother made my mother's full bridal outfits: all the dresses for my Mum and the bridesmaids." I had never known that, because it was before my time and there had never been any mention of this. I did know from conversations that earlier on Mum had been involved in embroidery and water colour painting. even claiming to have known Lloyd Rees. Again that was before my time.

Before she left for Rabaul, Mum was mentioned in a news article in the *Courier Mail* as being responsible for a spectacular flower display at some civic event. However, I know nothing of her creativity while in Rabaul. Maybe it all went into her work at the Legislative Assembly.

In New Guinea, Mum had four native servants called "boys" at that time. They were euphemistically termed indentured labour. Once I found an old faded sepia photo of these boys. Mum said, "Their names are written on the back.", So I turned over the photo to read their names, which were pencilled in, *House Boy, Cook Boy, Garden Boy, and All Purpose Monkey.* According to Mum it was alright to use the word, "monkey", Mum said that he was just like a car mechanic who can be called, "a grease monkey." I was not so sure.

After New Guinea, when we were old enough, my brother and I became her *de facto* servant boys, when required, which seemed to be most of the time. Unless it was a Saturday and we managed to escape from the house with the injunction, "Just be home before dark": a freedom many children today do not experience. For as long as I can remember, when Mum was too busy, or just not "up to it", we were responsible for house duties: cooking, clearing up, washing and drying the dishes, sweeping the polished floors, washing the clothes, hanging them out on the line. Only sometimes did we have to do the ironing, which Shane enjoyed. I did not. Once when Mum was doing the ironing she kept repeating, "I should not have to do this."

We were also responsible for the gardening, with Mum choosing the plants. I could grow vegetables of my own choice: mainly lettuces, beetroot, cabbages, silverbeet and spring onions. The task of cutting the grass became easier after an old friend gave us what was then a very recent invention, an electric lawn mower. Before that it was a scythe and the hard-to-push mower. With the electric mower, the only thing to be careful about was not to run over the cord and then pick it up. We never did. No primary kid in our street had an electric mower. The Victa Motor Mower days were yet to happen.

I remember on one occasion, when I must have been dodging tasks by reading, Mum appeared and declared, "God would be much happier, if you got out of that book and mowed the grass under your Mother's clothes line." Seemed to me rather amazing that she thought she actually knew what God was feeling. Strange but memorable.

We just assumed that we had to do all these tasks so Mum could get on with her "real work", which was whatever creative interest she had at the time. Our lives were different from other kids in our neighbourhood, but they all had fathers. We did not. Presumably that accounted for our different lifestyle. Our life was imagined by us to be as normal as any other family, except for the absence of a father.

Mum assumed we could do almost anything a man could do. When I was at secondary school, she discovered that she could get free exterior house paint from the Repatriation Department (usually simply called the Repat. and now known as Veterans Affairs). They would arrange for the loan of trestles, which was a necessary requirement, as our weather-board house was high up on 2 metre stumps at the front. Mum naturally chose vibrant colours. Shane and I painted the weather-boards turquoise, the windowsills and frames burgundy, and primrose yellow under the eaves. After that, all the other houses around looked even duller than they had before.

Our lives were saturated with a never-ending torrent of words; unless Mum was down, reading a book or stayed in bed. Then we looked after ourselves and the house was quiet for a while.

Mum was an avid, even voracious, reader. She claimed to have read every word published by Charles Dickens. Sometimes we seemed to have his characters wandering around the house. Of particular interest to Mum were *Great Expectations* Miss Havisham and Abel Magwitch, the convict returned to England.

If I had to choose a literary person who could be my role model, this would be Saul of ancient Israel. Saul's behaviours seem to me to be one of the oldest literary expressions of bipolar tendencies. At times the Spirit comes upon Saul and he is possessed with prodigious energy. Other times he sinks into depression. Ultimately Saul is deposed because he does not obey the alleged divine command to commit genocide. David sets about killing all his family, except one physically disabled son, who because of this will never be a regal threat to King David.

Interestingly Mum's sister, our Aunty Roma, claimed that Becky Sharp of *Vanity Fair* was her life model. To this day I believe this to have been so. Aunty Roma opened her tearooms with the name, *Becky's*. After, "my heroine", as she said. Unlike others in the Love family, Aunty Roma never showed any signs of bipolar tendencies.

As Shane and I were members of this wordy Love family, we missed school each fortnight to go to town. The educational purpose was for us to get our maximum number of eight books out of the biggest lending library in Brisbane, the *Brisbane School of Arts Library* in Ann Street. In fact in that era I can recall no other libraries in Brisbane, except for the very small State Library of Queensland beside the river near the Treasury Buildings, which was not a lending library. In Victoria our Great Aunt Elsie had a penny exchange lending library, I can recall none of these in Brisbane.

While in town, Mum would converse with old friends, acquaintances and strangers: in fact anyone she happened upon and who was prepared to converse with her. We usually went walking up and down Queen or Adelaide Streets. We'd window shop and be, "just looking" often inside the department stores of *Finney's* or *Allan and Stark's*. By noontime it would be lunch at the *Colony Club* or the *Shingle Inn.* Wonderfully the *Shingle Inn* still exists. Its interior relocated within the Brisbane City Hall and virtually unchanged from seventy years and more ago. After consuming the usual pie and peas for me, we went off to the Brisbane School of Arts Library. The words Mum used for our day in town was that it was, "for their education", which Mum would write in the required letter to the teacher in her copperplate script.

On one of these trips to town an over zealous salesman in Finney's, tried to sell something to Mum that she did not want. She said that she was, "just looking", but this did not deter the salesman. In exasperation she exclaimed that as far as she was concerned, he could, "just stick it!" When he persisted, she said, "Our conversation is now Bugauppinis." A well-dressed lady standing nearby said, "Really!" as we walked off.

Neighbours, oblivious to Cilla having a manic depressive condition, made it clear that at times they disapproved of her language. "You should not say that Cilla!" Well she did: acting out what would one day be the theme words of a television serial, "To boldly go where no man has gone before."

Her unconventional behaviour also came under judgements on many fronts. She did not stay at home and do house duties. Her boys were expected to do as much as her, if not more. Her boys did what should have 'traditionally' been a girl's or a mother's house task. This was still an era when the man alone was meant to be the "breadwinner" and a woman's place was in the home. Thankfully for us, Mum never abided by that. She did not care what they thought. If she had, we would have missed out on so many adventures that all the other kids in the street never experienced.

I remember one late afternoon, the sun going down, while we were out playing with other kids on the street. Suddenly, there was her penetrating voice calling us to tea with, "Kai Kai ready! Boys!"

Mum would take us to places where other children in our street never went. The highlight of the year was to go to Sydney for the long Christmas holidays. Once we flew by a Skymaster from Brisbane to Sydney. It was not long after the War and the terminal at Eagle Farm was a disused aircraft hanger with some canvas chairs for passengers to sit on.

When we arrived in Sydney at Mascot, we caught a multi-coloured taxi to Kings Cross. Mum knew the ropes. It was always, "Up the Cross, please." To say, "Kings Cross" was a giveaway: for the taxi driver who responded to the unsuspecting with a full tour all around Sydney: eventually by a tortuous route arriving at Kings Cross.

Gran was the live-in caretaker-manager of a four storey set of flats in Kings Cross Road, Kings Cross. Up the street in the Cross "proper", especially after dark, all was activity. Unlike Brisbane Town, the shops stayed open well into the night. There was so much to see: people dressed in funny clothes, men with long hair cuts, and drunks staggering around sometimes yelling funny things and what was then termed very rude words.

One night while we were walking in the cool evening air I said to Mum,
> "Why don't we go into *The Pink Pussy Cat*. The girls look wonderful only dressed in feathers."
> "No! You can't go in."

"Why not?"

"It leaves nothing to the imagination. That's my last word on the matter. Don't pester."

The last word with Mum was always rather tricky, because I usually did not know just when it was about to be announced.

Up at the Cross, New Year's Eve was just the best. By midnight it was bedlam. All the crowds everywhere. Each year we looked forward to that time in Sydney.

For the other holidays in the school year, we usually went somewhere in Queensland, mainly in the South East. As long as there was a national park nearby. Mum loved these places, especially where there was a rainforest.

We would go walking with her, sometimes on formed paths, other times pathless, "Just don't touch the stinging trees." Once on Mount Tamborine in wintertime, when it was a sunny day, we went on a walk down to a waterfall. The path was the only place where there were patches of sunlight. Here and there along the way some snakes had come out to get a little warmth. Mum said, "Just walk around them. You don't harm them: they won't harm you." And it was so.

On another occasion on the edge of Lamington National Park, she was wandering alone climbing up to a rocky overhang on the mountain, below the Lost World, when she came upon a large python, unexpectedly out in the day time, as they usually prefer to drop down from high up in the rainforest canopy after dark. She was thrilled. She had something new to talk about for weeks. I think she would have resonated with some words of the Aboriginal poet Samuel Wagan Watson,

like the snake that rushes before your feet
and you the only audience
a gift only for your eyes
from the old people
maybe
how do you know?

On other occasions when we were walking through the more open bush or in the rainforest it was always relentlessly, "Look at this!" "Look at that!" If Mum knew the botanical name, best we learn it. Once, on the edge of Lamington National Park, I found a tiny hoop pine seedling. I put it in an IXL Marmalade jam tin and took it home to plant beside the dunny. The dunny is long since gone and the tree now visible from a kilometre away, towering above other trees. Naturally I was required to refer to this tree as an *araucaria cunninghamii:* not hard to remember, as Cunningham was an explorer of some fame in Queensland and the Araucarians, a tribe in southern Chile that the Spanish took centuries to subjugate. The ancient species name may allude to the supercontinent of Gondwanaland.

In the midst of all this sometimes hyperactivity, it was never possible to know when Mum would go into a slump. We knew the reality far too well. Waiting for Gran to come and help us, while we did all the tasks and Mum was off to her room with all the blinds down and Mum in bed. We even had to empty the slops from the bucket she kept under the bed. Our lives were certainly different from the other kids in our street. Of some things Shane and I experienced, they never knew.

When she was up and about, the unexpected was always wonderful. Nakedness did not seem to bother her. Once she took us to the Queensland Art Gallery for the usual educational reasons, to broaden or minds and to increase our general knowledge. A wide general knowledge was as much prized as exam marks in Mum's estimation. At one point I was standing and staring at a full frontal naked young woman. Mum suddenly says, "That's very rude!" I was surprised, until she added, "Don't stare like that! Staring is rude!'

Sometimes it could be difficult to know what was the wrong that I had done, what crime inadvertently committed; not that I knew that word then. Once trouble came upon me after we had been to see family friends at Runcorn in a very opulent two storey house, where we were given a very good afternoon tea. I spent a lot of time looking at their beautifully illustrated art magazines that came from London. As in some special films of the day, these were in vivid technicolour. Going home on the train Mum said, to me, "You were a disgrace to the family." I thought I'd been on my best behaviour. "You stirred your cup of tea far too loudly." It was not always easy to get it right for Mum. However it was always good to be with her on another trip anywhere her whim took her, even if there might be trouble later because of my bad manners. This was a time when manners mattered very much indeed.

Time and tide – and Mum – never waited for anyone. If waiting was liable to be involved, the role of waiting in a queue was reassigned to Shane or me. This happened regularly on Pension Day. We became her authorised delegates to collect the money.

Not waiting for the train was another example of Mum's approach. She had a solution that seemed to be quite clever and reasonable, but a bit of a pain for me. In the forties after the War last century, the trains did not have automatic doors.

Each door had a big brass handle, which you turned to get the door open.

I have expressed in the words of a poem about this procedure thrust upon me. I imagined myself as a child when writing this recently. It may be doggerel, because of the corny rhymes and the fairly predictable metric pattern.

My Mum she doesn't have a car
And she doesn't like to wait
So when we go to catch the train
We always leave, a little late.

Half way up the road Mum says,
"Now you just run ahead
And hold the train for me."

So off I go, and know,
What trouble there will be.

Around the corner, down the steps,
Across the platform fast,
Just grab an open door and don't let go.
Just hold on till the last.

The guard: he gives a mighty shout,
That's easy to ignore.
The engine driver yells,
"Let go the bloody door!"
The stationmaster then appears,
In all his fancy clothes.
And he has met my Mum before.

She's someone that he knows.

He sighs, "Thank God! At last, you're here!"
As Mum comes gently down the stairs.
Gives a wicked smile and says, "Get on!
At Central we will pay our fares."

The station quickly slides away
And mum says, "Just settle down.
Read your comics quietly there,
And soon we'll be in town!"

One interest remained with Mum all her days. This was gardening. Shane and I were often the gardeners who did the digging, planting and weeding. Mum usually selected what was to be planted. Sometimes we were given packets of *Yates Garden Seeds*, with colourful pictures of the plants on them. Otherwise flowering plants and shrubs were grown from cuttings. These came from friends' gardens, or plants from any garden Mum had come across, which were reachable from the footpath. She always carried a pair of scissors in her hand bag, to be used for this purpose. She assumed the owners of the plants wouldn't mind, or said she'd, "known them for years." Either way she'd arrive home with cuttings that we had to nurture in a jar of water until roots sprouted or we put them straight into the ground and watered regularly, so that they eventually flourished. She had a particular obsession with collecting different varieties of hibiscus, frangipani and rose bushes.

Sometimes Mum went into a manic spending mood. She had very little money in her savings, basically depending solely on the regular Pension Payments. Shane remembers once being in the front yard when an unknown man drove up in a brand new Holden. He announced to Shane, "Just delivering Mrs Higgins' new car." We had to undo the agreement. Another time Mum came home in a happy mood to say, "I just put a lay-by on a beautiful new grand piano. Now I will be able to take up my piano playing again." It was not easy cancelling that and retrieving the money already laid down. This is still rather painful to remember and relate.

On another happier day of less expensive impulse buying, Mum arrived home with a portable gramophone. It was coloured pink and grey. There were two speakers which could be detached and separated by a yard (less than a metre) for a stereo effect. She also bought some 78 vinyl records including *March Militaire*, and *Scotland the Brave*, which she loved, music being very important to her.

While to so many others, Mum appeared to be so colourful and full of energy, again there would emerge that darker side to her, well-hidden from public view. Shane and I could tell when depression was about to cloud across her face. She began to go quiet. She would gradually fade into a world of silence, to wall herself into her prison of depression. The awfulness of such a prison is that not only does it imprison the depressed person, it also walls out those who want to help.

As time went on as she approached her sixties, the ups and downs became more frequent and more extreme. Once, in the middle of the night, having drunk too much water after tea, I was rushing out through the dining room to get to the little house – or "dunny", as we called it – up the back yard. I collided with Mum who was standing frozen there. I think the clinical phrase is "in a catatonic state". Eventually she woke up; became unfrozen and then got on with life as if nothing had happened. In fact before long, she was in a new upwards cycle.

Party Mode

Mum always
down in the dumps or
up in the clouds,
rarely in between
Full on or Full stop
That's the way she goes.

Tonight she's on a high,
A happy host of visitors:
Sherry, champagne, and cocktails
risqué jokes served with
homemade sausage rolls,
mock chicken, gherkins and cheese,
cheerios with tomato sauce
along with other savouries.

Amidst the scattered frangipani
Over a fine linen table cloth
through cigarette smoke clouds
Mum talks incessantly:
Fills our house
with words like nails
well hammered,
into
the double wooden walls.

While Mum's penetrating voice could be hard to take; her going quiet was far, far worse. To this day I abhor silence. When it falls around a dinner table, I impulsively say anything to break what I perceive as an icy silence.

There were aspects of Seasonal Affective Disorder for Mum and for me, though such a phrase was unknown to us at the time. As I do, Mum hated cold weather and grey skies with their depressing clouds. Such days did not necessarily precipitate rain but they so often precipitated Mum's descent into depression. Once the sky was dark, uniform grey with clouds that were not spectacular cumulonimbus, she could become quite depressed.

As a digression: usually if there was an approaching subtropical thunderstorm heralded by the rising magnificent brilliant white-topped cumulonimbus clouds, Mum was immediately energised. She delighted in lightning, thunder and rain. We would sit outside on our little top of the steps landing our miniature verandah, to look at the developing storm and discuss whether the lightning was chain, sheet or fork. We would regularly count the seconds between lightning flash and thunderclap, to judge how far the storm was and if it was coming closer, closer, or moving away. These times remain happy memories to recall. I love a thunderstorm.

However when the sky was overcast with louring clouds of a steely monochrome grey, Mum and the house inside became not only darker and very gloomy, she could remain that way for some days, sometimes with dishevelled hair. Thankfully in Brisbane – unlike in Melbourne – the grey skies do not come for long to stay, even in the wintertime.

Usually when the sun came out dazzling in the intense blue, Mum was up and out again. She never would have wished to be "beyond blue". Likewise for me: the bright blue skies are so important. Interestingly, recently David Coles, a paint manufacturer who moved from Manchester to Melbourne, described how in Australia he had to invent a new colour, Zinc Blue for artists to express the intense bright blue of our skies.

Sadly Mum's condition did not stay stable. In fact, as she moved into her early sixties her mood oscillations became more frequent and of greater intensity. The medication available to her was of little help in lessening the extremes of highs and lows. The bipolar condition is for life, for better or worse, gift and curse. In her day, not only was medication not very effective: from time to time she had to receive shock treatment, which made her dopey and confused for some time afterwards. Today a bipolar person like me can receive much more effective medical and psychological help.

As the years passed the extremes became more and more extreme and more frequent. I was appointed to a position in Warwick, some 100 miles away from our home in Brisbane and Shane became Mum's main carer, while he studied at the University.

When she committed suicide, she was sixty-four years old. After the funeral service in the Sherwood Presbyterian Church, so many of her old friends said they never had any idea that there was a dark, depressive side to her. "She was always so bright, so happy and colourful in all her ways." Or so they thought.

Now like them, despite the many painful memories of living with her bipolar condition, I love to remember her most colourful side.

A Colourful Life

Bright colours fascinate my Mum,
Loves vermilion, cyclamen,
Cerise and celadon.
Loves paintings by Van Gogh,
And Vlaminck as well.

Gives me a lovely paint tin:
So many colours in tiny tablets:
Black printed names,
Beneath every one.

Burnt ochre,
Prussian blue,
Burnt sienna,
Cobalt blue.

For me such colours
Never cease to fascinate,
Enthral, captivate.

Tropical flowers in bloom:
Blue or yellow butterflies:
Dragonflies too:
Bodies, Crimson or
Electric blue.

Like Mum, all the day
I see vivid colours,
On my way.
Little do I know,
One day they will say,
"Just like your Mum,
You're bipolar too."

The colours
Seen so bright,
Presage this day
Seventy years away.

When Mum committed suicide between Barbara's and my engagement and marriage in 1965, I did not cry, having learned not to, and maybe because of my bipolar emotional disconnectedness. Barbara said that when the right time came, then I would shed my tears. The right time came more than twenty years later.

It occurred during a coffee break in an academic conference at the Australian National University. A presenter, Margaret Reeson, showed me the list of all the "disappeared" in Rabaul: all those lost, male ex-pat Australians, the planters, the missionaries, the public servants of the Administration Centre at Rabaul.

I began reading this list. I started recognising name after name of friends and acquaintances Mum had spoken about for many years after the Pacific War, wondering what happened to them. Suddenly I felt an overwhelming sense of loss. I cried uncontrollably for my Dad, then over forty years dead. I also cried for my Mum.

CHAPTER XIX

LIVING WITH A BIPOLAR CONDITION: MY GRANDFATHER

In retrospect from fragments of information and my own observations before I was ten years old, I am inclined to believe that Grandpa Love (Mum's father) also suffered from a bipolar condition. I became aware that some things interested Grandpa a lot. Then suddenly he lost interest. Also he could go into very dark silent moods.

Once years before we lived next door, he had a very big chook run stretching over two thirds of the backyard. He built two chook houses. One seemed to be a fowls' version of the Taj Mahal. It was made of flattened out kerosene tins soldered together. Inside were sloping tiers of perches for the chooks to perch and sleep on and there was a wide, central, sandy floor. By the time we came to live beside Grandpa's house, all the chooks were gone. The yard inside the bigger yard remained with its high wire fence with horizontal wires at the top to stop any foxes getting in.

On rainy days this became another place to play, other than under the house. Here, before an audience of neighbouring kids, Shane held his famous World Premiere and simultaneously, the Finale performance of his *Naked Dancing Dick*. Sadly I was not present. When the event became known around the neighbourhood and one of the mothers heard, the locals were horrified and furious. I think Mum only pretended to be, as later she thought it was very funny.

In his last few years, when Grandpa was obviously in a manic mode, he was into making toys. This became his current obsession. Morning, noon and night he was sawing, planing, hammering and painting: accumulating a great number of wooden toys all made on his benches under his large Queenslander house. He made wooden steam trains, cars, blackboards, dolls and skittles. Then, apart from the ones he gave to us grandchildren, all of them were piled into his Hupmobile and taken to the City Mission. He had his photograph on the front page of *The Courier Mail*.

In a fairly regular pattern Grandpa went silently into himself, pulled down all the manilla blinds in his Queenslander and disappeared within: not to emerge for many days.

If he was manic we could go with him in his car, which was exhilarating, as he drove without any sense of speed limits, just tearing along with all the window flaps open, going as fast as he could go, *The Wind in the Willows* Mr Toad-style. "Pop, pop, pop!" He had various nicknames locally for this reckless behaviour, such as, *The Red Terror*. Mum did not like us going in his car but he would take us without telling Mum, which made her very angry, no doubt concerned for our safety.

Over a lifetime Grandpa had many interests. He was a surveyor by vocation. By about forty years of age through his prodigious energy, he had amassed enough money to retire and became a self-supporting gentleman naturalist. In his house could be found: cameras, theodolites, telescopes, microscopes, barometers and thermometers, along with scientific journals especially on Egyptology and a twenty-volume *Encyclopedia Britannica* set.

Mum said in the early days, when Grandpa was in an up mood, he'd get up before dawn and awaken all the family to hear the bird songs heralding the day. He had a great temper and neither his wife, nor his children would ever cross him without often long-term reprisals. I believe only Aunty Roma dared to. If one did, the punishment could be initially silence, then later, possibly for years; even reaching beyond his death into his will.

CHAPTER XX

LIVING WITH A BIPOLAR CONDITION: MY GREAT GRANDFATHER

Grandpa's behaviour could well have been replicating his father's, my Great Grandfather, Robert Alexander Love whose professional life seemed to oscillate between creativity and slumps. He was a very clever civil engineer as well as an architect of note. My reading of his biography, *A Victorian Goldfields Architect*, seemed to confirm the feeling that he too had a bipolar disability.

One often-told family story was about the time he was lecturing at the Bendigo School of Mines and Industries. One day he set off for work after breakfast, worked all day, then worked all night and returned home sometime the next morning, walking through the streets of Bendigo in full daylight carrying his still-lit lamp.

He was the restless wanderer: Ballymena, Northern Islandm to Edinburgh thence to New York, to Cincinnati, to San Francisco, to Melbourne, to Bendigo and then back to Cincinnati, where he died of Tuberculosis. Ironically, he was laid out in the very cemetery he had laid out many years before.

Examples of his creativity – in terms of architecture – still exist in houses in Bendigo, homesteads in the Western District of Victoria, St Matthew's Uniting Church in Stawell and St Paul's Anglican Cathedral in Bendigo.

Another aspect of his lasting heritage was disclosed to me in the words of a psychiatrist, "You did not stand much of a chance with that heavy genetic heritage." I believe that this is so. Close friends and relatives have said on occasions, "It runs in the family."

CHAPTER XXI

LIVING WITH MY BIPOLAR FOR MORE THAN FIFTY YEARS: BARBARA MY WIFE

Barbara, my wife of more than fifty years is another person who lives with the consequences of a bipolar disorder, namely mine. In our retirement this is usually 24/7.

My unpredictable mood changes must have been a great trial for her from the moment we were married. I was an impulsive, somewhat insensitive lover, companion and soul-mate. Neither of us realised that my ways of coping and not coping, were very strongly bipolar determined.

At this stage in my life of eighty years, I still like to be on the go. My doing things as fast as possible can become slap dash: the dishes washed in record time, but not spotlessly clean. Also my accelerating talking can presage my becoming just too manic, or as some family members say to this day, "A little bit high".

Up to the time of my hospitalisation, I would still head off in the car when I was elevated, blissfully unaware of how others in the car may have felt about my zipping along gaily. My behaviour echoed that of the Biblical King Jehu who, "drove his chariot furiously". To do this can be not just impulsive; it can be downright dangerous to myself and others.

After being full on, I would be fully down. And Barbara had to live with this as best she could, as I often sitting still in the lounge room, plodded through those valleys of deep darkness.

Along with my experiencing this Divine Presence, the other presence has been that of the other-centred, Barbara. She is always with me, to comfort me: so I need not fear any evil. From time to time, she will remind me that the depression never lasts for ever: even though at any time, its permanence seems to me to be a distinct possibility.

In our previous working lives, Barbara had breaks from me. A great deal of my time was expended in the energising environment of teaching religious education to students who often resented this compulsory activity in Uniting Church colleges. As well, there were preparations and celebrations, which included assembly devotions, chapel services and weddings. In these activities the manic side of my condition could be a great bonus. When I was down I could disappear into my Chaplain's room (not a Chaplin's Room, as a student once suggested).

However in our shared retirement, we are still learning to adjust. For the relief, or respite of us both, I religiously go on my after-breakfast, brisk, morning walk most days to the local *Flock Coffee Shop* or *The Little Bird,* for a coffee and to hopefully read a complimentary copy of a newspaper before hotfooting it home.

Sometimes when I am in full flight, Barbara obviously seeks to pull me gently like a kite in the wind, back to earth. Other times Barbara may seek to correct my fanciful version of what happened in my latest anecdote or story. Then a listener says, "Let him tell his story". Sometimes they even add words such as, "We love him as he is." Unlike Barbara they will not be present to witness this human kite crash down to earth, dropping like a duck shot on the wing.

Still as in Monty Python's, *Life of Brian*, Barbara often manages to, "look on the bright side of life". We enjoy going out to meals together, with close friends, or with our wider family. Then when I am elated, usually in a social setting, talking loudly, self-centredly and seemingly endlessly, Barbara, sometimes Geoff or Bronwyn, will suggest that I just settle down. My daughter Bronwyn may say, "Dad! Give someone else a go!" Or Geoff says, "You're talking too loudly, Dad." in his gentle way: which is so much easier to heed than such words as in a recent greeting, given as I approached the dinner table in a Red Hill restaurant. "Here comes the loudest megaphone on the Mornington Peninsula."

Barbara and the wider family have indeed been, and are for me, a blessing. This has been so all through decades of my bipolar behaviours. It is Barbara who has been prepared to, "stand by me", as in the title of a film the students loved. Together we have created a rich family life, which extends to our children, their spouses and all our seven grandchildren.

I believe now at more than eighty years, if Barbara had not steadfastly accompanied me thorough thick and thin, I could well have taken the road to suicide, which my Mother chose in her night of deep depression.

While not being of a Catholic persuasion, I wonder sometimes if I actually had a Guardian Angel beside me, when I engaged in my not-infrequent risk-taking actions. I recall once running crazily towards a sea cliff edge, ahead of our friends who were approaching very cautiously. As I peered over the fragile edge to the broken black basalt rocks far below, someone remarked, "He's courting death." Then adding, "I hope he does not marry her." So far I have not.

I have never had to survive the sad experiences of some others who presumably had a mental state similar to mine and discovered one day a family member had decided never to have anything to do with them again, because they, "just had enough". All the members of our family have always been caring. Also I have a wide circle of friends who understand my behaviours, and as best they can, accept me as I am.

For me having a bipolar condition has been both curse and blessing, as I presume also for Barbara: always having the possibility, or more correctly, the inevitability of often unexpected going up or down. This continues to happen capriciously, despite more than two and a half years of treatment, medical and psychological. Nowadays the cycles are much more gently up and down. They can last for months at a time, or a little shorter.

A certain self-awareness has been a priceless gift. Whenever things have gone a little out of kilter and later, I am back upon a less undulating way, like Don Quixote after one of his misadventures, I trust, "I know who I am."

CHAPTER XXII

CONCLUSION

To have spent three weeks locked up in the Aged Persons' Mental Health Unit at Frankston Hospital has been an invaluable, life-transforming experience. As I wrote earlier, in this Unit I learned the diagnosis of my condition and benefited from the healing of caring staff, who even made home visits for many months after my discharge. Also there has been prolonged psychological counselling locally at Positive Psychology.

Overall it has been, and still is, an exciting and colourful life. I still find it very hard to sit still for long, unless involved in conversation, reading, or writing. So I still have what Barbara once termed, *The Demented Grasshopper Syndrome*, which sadly is not in any official medical classification list yet! Hopefully this metaphor alludes to Leichhardt's grasshopper – "bright brick colour dotted with blue" – whose appearance heralds the Wet in the North of Australia with lightning and thunder. An alternative totem creature for me would be a red-eyed green tree frog from a Queensland rainforest.

A myriad of ideas still go swirling around in my restless mind in the middle of the night (or any time in the day) – buzzing like a swarm of bees. As in *Alice in Wonderland,* I am always, "curiouser and curiouser". Since a little child I have tried to walk in the way of Jesus of Nazareth. I live by the Monash University motto, *Ancora Imparo,* "I am still learning".

Traveling On (dedicated to my wife Barbara)

Now in these latter life days:
Wander westward,
Across the vast Darling Downs;
Under clear blue skies,
Through the savannah countryside.
Horizons wide, mountains far away,
Through blue gum, black iron bark,
Yellow box, and wattle:
Across the black soil plains:
Not true flatlands,
Just gently undulating:
Sometimes a little hill
Or grassy sandy ridges
Have to climb up and down:
Now and then a gully,
Down and up again,
Usually quite speedily.

Now eighty and more,
Still on medication;
The track leads ever on,
Towards my sunset:

Faster, faster,
Further further on,
From Goondiwindi westward
Red sand ridges
Rise endlessly ahead
As I travel on,
Always hopefully.

END NOTES

I have imitated a procedure used by Gerald Murnane, who somewhere in his recent *Border Districts,* declares that he relies on his memory when writing. What is not recallable, is presumably not memorable at all for him. So too with me in these memoirs.

This essay is really a kaleidoscope of memory fragments: some of them quite vivid, as colourful as the stained glass windows in the Sherwood Presbyterian Church of my childhood. They are also like Grandpa Love's beautiful glass panels from door height to floor level on either side of his most imposing front door at the end of the wide central hall of his classic Queenslander. These glass panels were lime green and raspberry. You could almost lick these clear coloured boiled lolly panes, which would cast their colours as seeming translucent light reflected on the polished floorboards of the long hall.

BOOKS OF SPECIAL INTEREST TO ME
IN THESE MEMOIRS INCLUDE:

Anne Therese Naylor, *Art from Adversity: A life with bipolar*

Gerald Murnane, *Border Districts* Giramondo 2017

Margaret Reeson, *A Very Long War: the families that waited.* Melbourne University Press 2000

Mike Butcher *Robert Alexander Love Goldfield Architect 1814-1876*

For, "Digressions being…" Laurence Sterne, *The Life and Opinions of Tristram Shandy, Gentleman. 759-67:* page 95 Penguin Paperback ed.

The phrase, "realms of gold", which is not infrequently used to express the worlds of literature, derives from the sonnet by John Keats, *On First Looking into Chapman's Homer.*

Jim Hawkins is the hero, in my opinion of R.L. Stevenson's *Treasure Island*, though some literary critics claim the hero is actually Long John Silver. Maybe they are both heroes, a doppelganger phenomenon.

For *The Epic of Gilgamesh.* I find the most literary-poetic version to be the Penguin Classics translation by N.K. Sandars first pub. 1960

Kenneth Grahame *The Wind in the Willows* page 200 (Oxford's Children's Classics)

Sarah Lodge, *Inventing Edward Lear* alludes at various times to his sudden mood changes and Lear's use of colours to convey emotional reactions.

Other significant books for me include: *Don Quixote, Alice in Wonderland* and the *Bible.*

EXTRA NOTES

1. "Dago" appears to be derived from the Spanish word, "Diego" a form of James. Dago was used in Australia all throughout the 20th century but became very commonly used during the period when refugees from the Mediterranean arrived in Australia after the Second World War.

2. Apollo is a complex god in Greek mythology. He is a god with many roles including: healing (as in the epithet, "Avertor of evil"), protector of sailors, sun and light, truth, prophecy and poetry.